CAMPAIGN 344

JAVA SEA 1942

Japan's Conquest of the Netherlands East Indies

MARK STILLE

ILLUSTRATED BY JIM LAURIER

Series Editor Marcus Cowper

OSPREY PUBLISHING
Bloomsbury Publishing Plc

Kemp House, Chawley Park, Oxford OX2 9PH, UK
29 Earlsfort Terrace, Dublin 2, Ireland
1385 Broadway, 5th Floor, New York, NY 10018, USA
Email: info@ospreypublishing.com
www.ospreypublishing.com

OSPREY is a trademark of Osprey Publishing Ltd

First published in Great Britain in 2019
Transferred to digital print in 2024

A catalogue record for this book is available from the
British Library.

Print ISBN: 978 1 4728 3161 3
ePub: 978 1 4728 3162 0
ePDF: 978 1 4728 3163 7
XML: 978 1 4728 3164 4

Maps by www.bounford.com
3D BEVs by The Black Spot
Index by Alan Rutter
Typeset by PDQ Digital Media Solutions, Bungay, UK
Printed and bound in Great Britain by CPI (Group) UK Ltd,
Croydon CR0 4YY

24 25 26 27 28   10 9 8 7 6 5 4

The Woodland Trust
Osprey Publishing supports the Woodland Trust, the UK's leading
woodland conservation charity.

www.ospreypublishing.com
To find out more about our authors and books visit our
website. Here you will find extracts, author interviews, details of
forthcoming events and the option to sign-up for our newsletter.

CONTENTS

The Philippines, Malaya, and the Netherlands East Indies, December 1941

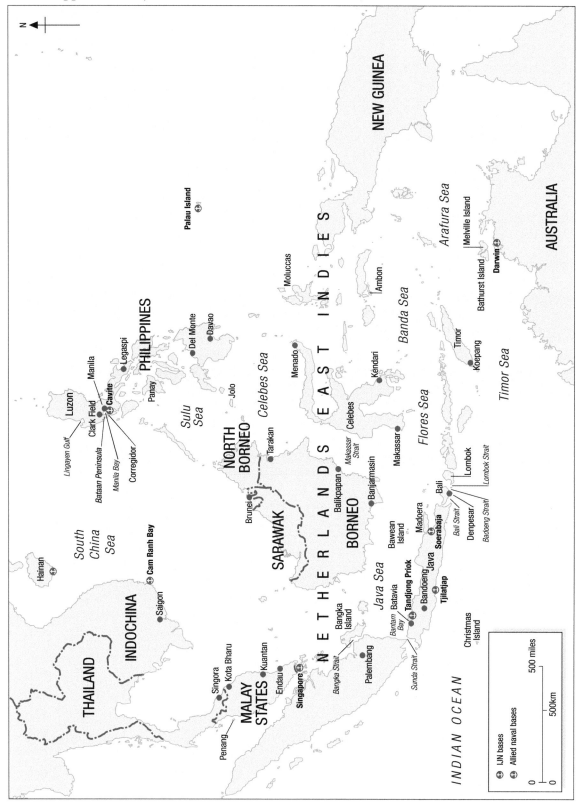

ORIGINS OF THE CAMPAIGN

The Japanese conquest of Southeast Asia during the initial period of the Pacific War, which included the naval battle of the Java Sea and a number of associated engagements, was the culmination of a train of events begun in the previous decade. The 1930s witnessed a wave of Japanese expansion in Asia. Japan's initial focus was on China because it was weak. In September 1931, the Japanese Kwantung Army occupied Manchuria. The following year, the Japanese prime minister was assassinated by a group of naval officers and army cadets which began a string of events leading to the end of civilian-controlled governments. This meant there were no internal curbs on Japanese expansionist ambitions.

In July 1937, fighting flared in northern China which led to a Japanese invasion of northern and coastal China. Despite massive Japanese gains in 1938 and the commitment of 1.5 million soldiers, the war in China became a stalemate. In 1939, war broke out in Europe which brought more opportunity and temptation for Japan's military leaders. Japan took a wait-and-see attitude to the European conflict, but by 1940 the Allied powers were on the ropes. With France and the Netherlands defeated, and the survival of the United Kingdom in doubt, the Japanese began to prepare for a war of expansion in the Far East.

The focus of this renewed war of expansion was Southeast Asia and its resources. The Imperial Japanese Army (IJA) supported a move south as a means to complete the isolation of China. The Imperial Japanese Navy (IJN) also supported expansion into Southeast Asia, because only the resources located there offered the means to withstand American economic pressure. Though unwilling to intervene against Japanese aggression in China, the United States did ratchet up economic pressure in response to continued Japanese expansion in China.

The virtually defenseless condition of the Netherlands East Indies (NEI) and the perilous condition of the British in Southeast Asia seemed to offer the Japanese a way out of their predicament with the United States. The Japanese economy was heavily dependent on American oil and scrap iron exports. Efforts to break the American economic stranglehold by negotiation were doomed to failure, since the Japanese would never voluntarily relinquish their conquests in China. Another factor driving Japan to war in the near term was the favorable naval balance compared to the US Navy in 1941 and 1942. Since the fruits of the United States' Two-Ocean Naval Expansion Act of June 1940 would place the IJN in a position of perpetual inferiority by early 1943, the window of opportunity for a successful war was fairly small.

Thus, the IJN assumed the role as the leading proponent of war against Great Britain and its empire, the Dutch, and the United States. In the mind of the Japanese, there was no way the United States would remain neutral if Japan attacked into Southeast Asia, so any war of aggression would also have to be waged against the United States. The groundwork for war in the Pacific was laid.

The immediate events leading to war are well known. In July 1941, the Japanese forced the Vichy French to declare a joint Franco-Japanese protectorate over Southeast Asia. In response, the Americans, British, and Dutch imposed a total trade embargo on the Japanese and froze all Japanese assets. Since there was no realistic prospect that a Japanese government dominated by the military would accede to American demands to withdraw from China or Indochina, the countdown to war accelerated. Japan had to act before its supplies of oil dwindled. Accordingly, the IJN demanded in August that hostilities against the Western Powers begin in October. The IJA agreed only two weeks later. A conference between the IJA and IJN on September 3 set the timeline for war. The rush to war was temporarily suspended by the Emperor's demand that diplomacy be given time to work, but by December 1 an imperial conference confirmed the decision for war.

THE NAVAL BALANCE OF POWER

Underpinning Japanese hopes for a quick victory was the balance of naval power which existed in December 1941. As the table below clearly shows, this balance favored Japan.

Pacific Naval Balance, December 7, 1941

	Battleships/ Battlecruisers	Aircraft Carriers	Heavy Cruisers	Light Cruisers	Destroyers	Submarines
Royal Navy and Dominions	2	0	1	8	12	1
Royal Netherlands Navy	0	0	0	3	7	15
US Navy Asiatic Fleet	0	0	1	2	13	29
US Navy Pacific Fleet	8	3	12	9	67	27
Allied Totals	10	3	14	22	99	72
IJN	10	10	18	20	112	65

British and Dutch naval forces, even with the assistance of the US Navy's Asiatic Fleet, were clearly inadequate to defend their Southeast Asian possessions. The inferiority of US Navy forces deployed in the Pacific against the IJN is also evident, which made any American attempt to move into the Western Pacific to relief the Philippines impossible.

The bedrock of British strategic planning to defend Malaya and Singapore was the assumption that significant naval reinforcements would be moved to the Far East shortly after the outbreak of hostilities. As hostilities seemed imminent in late 1941, the British made good on their promise to send naval reinforcements to defend Malaya. However, this reinforcement was nothing more than a bluff in an attempt to deter the Japanese from opening hostilities.

The move was the brainchild of Prime Minister Winston Churchill, who contended that the dispatch of a small but powerful striking force would give the Japanese pause. The force which finally arrived in Singapore on December 2 was comprised of the modern battleship *Prince of Wales*, the old battlecruiser *Repulse*, and a mere four destroyers. The force was designated as Force Z and placed under the command of acting Admiral Sir Tom Phillips.

The US Navy's Asiatic Fleet, under the command of Admiral Thomas Hart, was caught in an exposed position when the war began. Its largest unit, the heavy cruiser *Houston* was at Panay, beyond the range of Japanese air attack, but five destroyers, all but two of the submarines, and most of the fleet's auxiliaries were in Manila Bay on December 8. Four of Hart's destroyers were actually on the way to reinforce the British in Singapore when war broke, arriving there on the morning of December 10.

This view was taken from *John D. Ford* of two other Asiatic Fleet destroyers in 1938 conducting one of the fleet's few open ocean operations. The Asiatic Fleet's combatants were deployed primarily for presence missions and training for their potential wartime missions was not a priority. (US Naval History and Heritage Command)

THE INITIAL JAPANESE ATTACKS

The initial scope of the Japanese offensive in the Pacific was breathtaking and far beyond what the Allies thought possible. The most audacious was the Pearl Harbor operation, in which the six fleet carriers of the Striking Force (Kido Butai) attacked the US Navy Pacific Fleet's primary base in

Hawaii. Gaining total surprise, two waves of Japanese aircraft exacted a terrible toll on the unprepared Americans. In total, 18 US Navy ships were sunk or damaged, including all eight of the battleships present. None of the Pacific Fleet's three carriers were present, and thus all survived. In the Western Pacific, Guam was invaded and quickly fell to the Japanese on December 10. The only Japanese misstep occurred on December 11, when an attempt to invade Wake Island in the Central Pacific was repelled by the American garrison. The Japanese returned in greater force on December 23 and successfully occupied the island.

In Southeast Asia, the Japanese quickly disproved the Allied assessment that they were capable of only a single invasion at a time. After crippling American airpower in the Philippines on the ground on December 8, the Japanese turned their attention to the Asiatic Fleet's main base at Cavite in Manila Bay on December 10 with a raid by 51 bombers. These proceeded to lay waste to the naval base. The bombs destroyed much of the navy yard with its repair and machine shops, parts and other stores to keep the fleet in fighting order. Submarine *Sealion*, in overhaul, was destroyed, and *Seadragon* was damaged. More importantly, most of the fleet's replacement submarine torpedoes were lost. Destroyers *Pillsbury* and *Peary*, also undergoing overhaul, were damaged. Despite the fact that both destroyers and all the major auxiliaries were able to depart Manila and head south over the next few days, the raid demonstrated clearly that Hart's plans of at least operating the submarines out of Manila were impossible. The fleet headed south, not to exposed Singapore, but to northwest Australia.

Having gained control of the air, the Japanese conducted a series of landings in the Philippines. These began on December 8 with a small landing on the island of Batan some 125 miles north of Luzon. A landing on the island of Camiguin, between Luzon and Batan, and at Aparri on northern Luzon followed on the 10th. On December 12, a landing at Legaspi in southern Luzon went off smoothly. The main landing at Lingayen Gulf took place on December 22. These operations completely outmaneuvered the defenders and forced the Americans to retreat into the Bataan Peninsula. Here, the Americans and Filipinos held out until April, and the last of the defenders did not surrender until Corregidor Island fell on May 6. Though their actions were ultimately futile, the American defenders in the Philippines held out much longer than their British counterparts in Singapore or the Dutch in the NEI.

Concurrently with their opening moves against the Philippines, the Japanese also invaded northern Malaya and southern Thailand. On December 8, Japanese troops conducted landings at Singora and Patani in southern Thailand and Kota Bharu in northern Malaya. Once established ashore, the Japanese 25th Army defeated the British at the battle of Jitra on December 11, which decided the fate of northern Malaya. By early January, central Malaya was lost when the Japanese smashed two Indian brigades at the battle of Slim River. By January 25, the British had decided to retreat back onto Singapore Island. The Japanese attacked across the Johore Strait on February 8 and a week later forced the garrison to surrender.

THE DESTRUCTION OF FORCE Z

On December 10, the Allied naval position in Southeast Asia took a dramatic turn for the worse. In response to the initial Japanese invasion of northern

The Japanese air raid on Cavite Navy Yard on December 10 eliminated it as a facility capable of servicing the Asiatic Fleet. This view shows the result of the raids with fires burning and heavy smoke. The submarine bow visible at the far right is probably *Sealion*, which had been hit by bombs and had settled by the stern. (US Naval History and Heritage Command)

This Japanese photograph shows Force Z under attack on December 10. *Prince of Wales* is moving at speed at the bottom of the photograph and *Repulse* at the top of the image is surrounded by bomb explosions. The destruction of these two capital ships changed the naval balance in Southeast Asia. (US Naval History and Heritage Command)

Malaya and southern Thailand, the aggressive Phillips decided to commit his small striking force to defeat the Japanese invasion. Phillips sortied from Singapore after dusk on December 8 with his entire force. He calculated that by using the monsoon weather to provide cover, he had a good chance to strike the Japanese landing force at Singora. The target was later changed to Kota Bharu, where Phillips hoped to engage the Japanese invasion force on the morning of December 10. Unfortunately for the British, any chance of surprise was quickly lost. A Japanese submarine spotted the force at 1345hrs on December 9 and Japanese aircraft picked up the force at 1740hrs.

About two hours later, Force Z came within some 22 miles of the IJN force, which was searching for it in the hope of engaging the British in a night action. At about the same time, Phillips decided to abandon the operation and head back to Singapore. However, at 2355hrs, a report reached the admiral that the Japanese had landed at Kuantan, which was then about 120 miles from Force Z's position. Phillips changed course to the southwest to investigate the report. Arriving at 0800hrs, Phillips sent an aircraft from *Prince of Wales* and a destroyer to investigate. They found nothing since the report was entirely false. Instead of resuming his transit south to the relative safety of Singapore, Phillips decided to investigate another false report of some barges off Kuantan. This proved to be a fatal delay.

The British were totally ignorant of the threat to Force Z posed by land-based IJN aircraft. They assessed that if they stayed 400 miles from the nearest Japanese airfield they would be beyond the range of effective attack. Even if the Japanese managed to hit Force Z, it would be only with high-level bombers like the British were accustomed to in the Mediterranean, and not the much-more-deadly torpedo aircraft. On both accounts, British intelligence was grossly inaccurate. Japanese G3M "Nell" and G4M "Betty" aircraft flying from airfields around the Saigon area had the range to strike as far south as Singapore itself. Both types of aircraft could carry the reliable Type 91 aerial torpedo, and their highly trained crews were also capable of hitting maneuvering ships with bombs from 10,000ft. The IJN massed a large force of long-range attack aircraft in Indochina with the mission of neutralizing Force Z. On December 10, a total of 85 G3M and G4M aircraft took off between 0625 and 0800hrs to find and attack Force Z.

Just as fuel was becoming critical for the Japanese, a reconnaissance aircraft sighted Force Z at 1015hrs. The first of the strike groups sighted the British ships at 1100hrs and began the first of a series of attacks. Eight G3M bombers made a level attack on *Repulse* and scored a single hit, which caused minor damage. The next attack by 17 G3Ms carrying torpedoes decided the outcome of the battle. Eight went after *Prince of Wales* and scored two hits. One of these doomed the battleship. It struck abeam the rear 14in. gun turret and caused the outer propeller shaft to buckle and several compartments to flood. The resulting flooding caused an 11.5-degree list and reduced speed to 15 knots. The other torpedo-carrying G3Ms went after *Repulse*, but the old battlecruiser dodged all nine torpedoes, as well as the bombs from another six aircraft. The next wave featured eight G3Ms which all launched their torpedoes at *Repulse*; again, the well-handled battlecruiser emerged unscathed. The following wave of 26 G4Ms with torpedoes delivered the coup de grace to Force Z. Six attacked *Prince of Wales*, which was unable to maneuver; four hits were recorded. Twenty G4Ms went after *Repulse*. This time, the attackers executed a pincer attack that placed five torpedoes on the battlecruiser. Unable to take this type of damage, the ship sank at 1233hrs with the loss of 513 men.

The fate of *Prince of Wales* was certain. A 1,100-pound bomb hit was scored by the last group of G3Ms to attack. The bomb penetrated the main deck where it exploded causing severe casualties. The battleship continued to settle and at 1315hrs, the crew was ordered to abandon ship. Five minutes later the ship capsized to port with the loss of 327 of her crew. In return for this brilliant attack, the Japanese lost three aircraft and 21 aircrew. The destruction of Force Z removed the only significant Allied naval force in Southeast Asia. With British naval power crippled and American air power in the Philippines neutralized, the only force left to prevent a Japanese invasion of the NEI was a scratch joint force of American, Australian, British and Dutch surface combatants. Its ability to defend the NEI would soon be tested.

CHRONOLOGY

1941

December 8	Japanese conduct landings at Kota Bharu, Malaya and at Singora and Patani, Thailand.
December 10	Force Z destroyed by Japanese land-based aircraft.
December 16	Japanese land at Miri, British Borneo.

1942

January 10	ABDA Command established.
January 11	Japan declares war on NEI.
	Japanese land at Menado, Kema, and Bangka Roads in the Celebes.
January 12	Japanese occupy Tarakan, Dutch Borneo.
January 23	Japanese land at Balikpapan, Dutch Borneo.
January 24	US Navy destroyers conduct raid on Balikpapan invasion force.
	Japanese occupy Kendari in the Celebes.
January 3	Japanese occupy Ambon Island.
February 2	ABDA Strike Force established.
February 4	Battle of the Makassar Strait.
February 14–17	Battle of the Bangka Strait.
February 15	Singapore surrenders.
	Japanese capture Bangka Island and Palembang, Sumatra.
February 16	Japanese occupy Bandjermasin, Dutch Borneo.

February 18	Japanese occupy Bali.
February 19	Battle of the Badoeng Strait.
	Japanese carrier force conducts raid on Port Darwin, Australia.
February 20	Japanese land on Timor Island.
February 27–March 1	Battle of the Java Sea.
February 28–March 1	Battle of the Sunda Strait.
March 8	NEI Surrenders.
March 28	Japanese complete occupation of Sumatra.

OPPOSING COMMANDERS

JAPANESE COMMAND STRUCTURE AND COMMANDERS

The Combined Fleet, which controlled all the IJN's important elements, was commanded by **Admiral Yamamoto Isoroku.** He may have been one of the few senior Japanese command figures who clearly foresaw the outcome of a war between the United States and Japan, but he was fully onboard for a war of aggression in Southeast Asia and made no attempt to address the probably dubious assumption that an attack against British and Dutch colonies would bring the United States into the war. His Pearl Harbor attack guaranteed that the United States would enter the war and foreclosed the possibility of a negotiated peace. Yamamoto's meddling late in the NEI campaign presented the weak Allied naval forces with an opportunity they were unable to exploit.

Yamamoto allocated the bulk of the Combined Fleet to conduct the campaign in Southeast Asia. Given the name Southern Expeditionary Force, it was commanded by **Vice Admiral Kondo Nobutake.** In peacetime, he was the commander of the Second Fleet. By all accounts,

ABOVE LEFT
Rear Admiral Tanaka was one of the IJN's most accomplished destroyer commanders. His fighting career began in the NEI campaign, but he went on to greater success during the Guadalcanal campaign. (US Naval History and Heritage Command)

ABOVE RIGHT
Rear Admiral Nishimura commanded one of the IJN destroyer squadrons in the NEI campaign. As such, he was given command of some of the many invasion operations at various points in the campaign. During the invasion of Balikpapan, he was responsible for overseeing the only Japanese naval defeat of the campaign. (US Naval History and Heritage Command)

he was a capable and aggressive commander. His success in leading the Southeast Asia campaign led to future important assignments until his failure at Guadalcanal. After Guadalcanal, he was never given another seagoing command.

The two pincers of the Japanese attack on the NEI were commanded by vice admirals. The Eastern Force was under the direction of **Vice Admiral Takahashi Ibo.** Takahashi is little known among the IJN admirals of the Pacific War, but began the war as the commander of the Third Fleet. Following his lackluster performance in the NEI, he remained in the region as Commander of the Southwestern Area Fleet until November 1942 after which he was relegated to lesser commands. He was arrested by American occupation authorities in December 1945 as a possible war criminal.

Takahashi's Eastern Force included powerful elements like **Rear Admiral Takagi Takeo's** Sentai (Squadron) 5 of heavy cruisers. Takagi had a background in cruisers and battleships and had assumed flag rank in November 1938, taking command of Sentai 5 in September 1941. He commanded the Eastern Force's covering force throughout the NEI campaign. At Java Sea, he was responsible for a sloppy force disposition which showed a lack of regard for the enemy, though overconfidence among Japanese admirals was not limited to Takagi. Following the conquest of the NEI, he commanded the Striking Force for the Coral Sea operation, which resulted in a Japanese defeat, and then participated in the disastrous Midway operation in June 1942. In June 1943, he was given command of the IJN's submarine command, the Sixth Fleet. When the Americans invaded Saipan in June 1944, Takagi was caught on the island and killed in action. The Eastern Force was assigned two destroyer squadrons whose commanders were given command of invasion convoys during the campaign. **Rear Admiral Tanaka Razio** commanded Destroyer Squadron 2. Tanaka went on from the NEI campaign to gain greater fame as a destroyer commander in the Guadalcanal campaign where he performed well, especially at the battle of Tassafaronga in November 1942. Ironically, he was held in higher esteem by the US Navy than by the IJN and, after being wounded in December 1942 when his flagship was sunk on a resupply mission, he was removed from command probably because of his pessimistic comments regarding the course of the campaign. Even though he was later promoted to vice admiral, he was never given another important command. **Rear Admiral Nishimura Shoji** commanded Destroyer Squadron 4. He had a poor record during the war and is mostly known for his last battle, when he commanded a force of old battleships during the battle of Leyte Gulf during which he was killed. His background was mostly in destroyers, and he assumed command of Destroyer Squadron 4 on May 1, 1940. His performance during the NEI campaign was spotty, but he retained his command at Midway and later commanded heavy cruisers at Guadalcanal.

The Western Force was under the command of **Vice Admiral Ozawa Jisaburo.** He is most commonly known as an airpower advocate and as the commander of the IJN's carrier force from November 1942 to November 1944, during which he commanded Japanese forces at the battle of the Philippine Sea. At the start of the war, he was given command of this important force and mission since he was held in high regard as a tactician and as a fighting leader. Ozawa was the last commander of the Combined Fleet before the end of the war in 1945.

The principal combatant force element under Ozawa was Sentai 7, commanded by **Rear Admiral Kurita Takeo.** He commanded the support force for the invasion of Java and was caught with his forces out of position during the last days of the campaign as the Allied naval forces fled the island. He went on to fight well at Guadalcanal and later Philippine Sea, but is best known for his refusal to commit the bulk of the IJN's remaining large ships to a futile operation to attack the American beachhead at Leyte in October 1944. **Rear Admiral Hara Kenzaburo** was Commander of Destroyer Squadron 5. He performed poorly in the last segment of the campaign and was relegated to second-tier positions after he gave up command of his squadron in March 1942.

The IJN's land-based air force played an important part in the campaign. **Vice Admiral Tsukahara Nishio** commanded the 11th Air Fleet which he assumed command of in September 1941.

Vice Admiral Ozawa was selected for the important assignment of conducting the invasions of Malaya, Sumatra, and western Java. His Malaya Unit performed well during the campaign, and his adept use of naval air power showed his background as an airpower advocate. He was an officer of great ability and later assumed command of the IJN's carrier force and the Combined Fleet. (US Naval History and Heritage Command)

Admiral Thomas Hart reads his orders to assume duties as commander of the Asiatic Fleet on July 25, 1939 aboard heavy cruiser *Augusta* at Shanghai, China. Hart was a very capable commander but enjoyed a short career as commander of ABDA naval forces. Given the forces at his disposal, it was never possible for him to accomplish his missions. He was scapegoated by MacArthur for unsuccessfully defending the Philippines and undermined by the Dutch because they felt that they should have the role as commander of ABDA naval forces. (US Naval History and Heritage Command)

ALLIED COMMAND STRUCTURE AND COMMANDERS

Despite their common threat, the Americans, British, Dutch, and Australians were unable to establish a working joint command before the war, and even after the war began still struggled to do so. In April 1941, the Americans, Dutch, and British held staff talks in Singapore (with Australian and New Zealand representatives in attendance), but these talks failed to create a working relationship. It took a high-level conference between Churchill and Roosevelt in December 1941–January 1942 to hammer out an agreement on a joint command structure in Southeast Asia. One of the agreements of the Arcadia Conference was the establishment of a joint command responsible for defending Allied possessions in Southeast Asia. The Americans proposed a structure for complete command of all naval, ground, and air forces in the region and put forward British **General Archibald Wavell** as its first commander. Despite some reservations on the potential effectiveness of a command covering such a large area and with restrictions imposed by the Americans, the British agreed to the establishment of ABDA (American, British, Dutch, and Australian) Command under Wavell's control. It covered all of the NEI, the Philippines, Malaya, and Burma. The Dutch and Australians were not consulted about its creation and Americans and Britons held almost all the important command positions.

Wavell's deputy was **Lieutenant-General George Brett**, US Army Air Force (USAAF) and his chief of staff was British officer **Lieutenant-General Sir Henry R. Pownall.** American **Admiral Thomas Hart** retained his national command and was appointed as commander of ABDA naval forces (also called ABDAFLOAT). Another American, **Major-General Lewis H. Brereton,** USAAF, was given the job as the commander of ABDA air forces until the arrival of another British general. ABDA ground forces were commanded by Dutch **Lieutenant-General Hein ter Poorten.** ABDA Command was largely ineffective from its first official day on January 15, 1942 until its final disbandment on February 25, when Wavell resigned.

The Allied naval command structure had the appearance of being streamlined, since it featured a single operational commander. In reality, Hart exercised limited operational command over the naval forces of the principal contributors. British naval forces remained focused on protecting convoys to Singapore while the Asiatic Fleet remained focused on protecting the eastern NEI and protecting convoys from Australia. This left the Dutch Navy to guard the center of the operating area which was beyond its means.

The Dutch were especially affected by the command arrangement since they were excluded from senior command positions and often found their forces being used to escort convoys into Singapore. In their view, they had the most to lose and were contributing a major portion of Allied naval forces, but had little say on how their forces were employed.

Admiral Hart was the commander of the Asiatic Fleet. He assumed this post 30 months before the war, so he knew exactly how limited his force's capabilities were. At the start of the Pacific War, he had over 40 years of

BELOW LEFT
Rear Admiral William Glassford, shown here in the 1930s, assumed command of the Task Force 5 before the Pacific War. Hart did not believe he was aggressive enough, as did many of his men, but he did oversee the Asiatic Fleet's only victory over the Japanese at the battle of Balikpapan. (US Naval History and Heritage Command)

BELOW RIGHT
Vice Admiral Helfrich photographed in 1945. Helfrich's aggressive determination to defend Java against tremendous odds made him the most important and controversial Allied naval command figure of the campaign. (Netherlands Institute for Military History)

service (being a graduate of the Naval Academy in 1897) and was one of the most senior admirals in the US Navy. His personality was summed up by his nickname "Tough Tommy." While seen as a strict disciplinarian, he was also viewed as fair. He proved adept at dealing with his command's pre-war responsibilities of protecting US economic and military interests in the Far East.

When Hart took over command of ABDA naval forces, day-to-day responsibilities for the operations of the Asiatic Fleet were transferred to his chief of staff **Rear Admiral W. R. Purnell. Rear Admiral William Glassford, Jr.** was given command of Task Force 5, the Asiatic Fleet's surface striking force. He was given the nickname "15-knot Glassford" in recognition of his hesitant leadership early in the war. He did not get along with Hart who did not think he was aggressive enough. When Hart assumed his role as ABDAFLOAT, the US Navy wanted him to hand over command of the Asiatic Fleet to Glassford. Hart avoided doing so until January 25, when Glassford found out about the order. When he had the opportunity to appoint a commander for the new ABDA Striking Force commander, Hart selected somebody else besides Glassford.

Hart's tenure as ABDAFLOAT was brief and was marked by political assaults from General Douglas MacArthur and the Dutch authorities. By February 5, **Admiral Ernest King**, Commander-in-chief of the US Fleet, informed Hart that he should ask to be relieved on health grounds since he had lost the support of the Dutch, MacArthur, Wavell, and even President Roosevelt. His relief was driven by MacArthur and the Dutch, who wanted to scapegoat him for the failure to defend the NEI. As of February 12, the position of ABDAFLOAT was held by a Dutch admiral. With the departure of Hart, there was not a single American naval officer with a significant role in ABDA Command.

Vice Admiral Conrad E. L. Helfrich was the commander of Dutch naval forces. He was born in the NEI and so had a special interest in its defense. His sea and command time was limited, but he returned to the NEI in 1931 and by 1939 he was named commander of East Indies Naval Forces and promoted to vice admiral the next year. He was bitter when Hart was named ABDAFLOAT instead of himself and he failed to cooperate with Hart and immediately began a campaign to undermine him. Hart's headquarters was not collocated with Helfrich's in Batavia, the Dutch naval base on western Java, and Hart essentially ignored him. Helfrich could only track ABDA naval operations through a liaison officer at Hart's headquarters. Helfrich returned the favor by being as uncooperative as possible with Hart, especially when it came to making Dutch ships available for operations. This changed when Hart left the NEI and turned over command to Helfrich on February 12. Helfrich was the key player in the later stages of the naval campaign in the NEI. He was a complex figure and ranged from being an arrogant bully to a reliable member of the Allied command team. His overriding instinct was to be as aggressive as possible in attacking the invading Japanese. This aggression became irrational in the later part of the campaign when he sacrificed not only Dutch but American, British, and Australian lives in a futile defense of Java. After directing much futile bloodshed, he escaped from Java by air to assume the paper position of Commander of Dutch Naval Forces in the Far East for the remainder of the war.

Tactical command of Dutch naval forces and later command of ABDA's Combined Striking Force when it was established on February 1 was given to **Rear Admiral Karel W. F. M. Doorman**. He was a 1910 graduate of the Royal Netherlands Naval College and became a naval aviator in 1915. After a Naval Staff College tour and various command tours on destroyers and cruisers, he was appointed commander of the Naval Air Service on the NEI. This was followed by a promotion to flag rank in May 1940 and the assumption of the command of the East Indies Squadron. Doorman is a difficult figure to assess, especially in light of his actions during the campaign. He was undoubtedly competent and respected by his peers and subordinates in the Royal Netherlands Navy. He could be charming and showed obvious care for the men under his command.

Days after being appointed commander of the Combined Striking Force, he led an ill-fated operation to attack Japanese shipping at Makassar. In consultation with Hart, he selected a direct route to the target and was subjected to intense air attack. Two American cruisers were damaged, with heavy casualties and Doorman was rattled by the affair. Doorman subsequently aborted another operation to attack an invasion convoy after being subjected to air attack. By the eve of the Java Sea battle, the other Allied naval commanders were fed up with Doorman. He had achieved nothing in his tenure as commander of the Striking Force and had "run away" on several occasions. There was even talk of replacing him on the eve of the battle, but in the end it was judged unwise to replace the commander at such a late stage, so Doorman remained in charge. Under pressure from Helfrich, and perhaps determined to allay fears he was not a fighter and to defend his homeland, at the battle of the Java Sea he displayed a real tenacity to close with and defeat the Japanese, whatever the cost. Few admirals during the war showed the same degree of determination. This determination came at the price of the destruction of his command which has led to his post-war reputation as being brave but stupid. He deserved better then and now, since he was caught in an impossible situation commanding an inferior force trying to carry out the orders of his superior officer who had little consideration for the men under his command.

British naval forces were initially under the command of acting **Admiral Tom Phillips** until his death on his flagship *Prince of Wales* on December 10. **Vice Admiral Geoffrey Layton** took back his old job as commander of the Eastern Fleet upon the death of Phillips. British naval units in the ABDA area were technically under the command of the Eastern Fleet. Layton remained in this position until March, when **Vice Admiral Sir James Somerville** arrived with reinforcements for the Eastern Fleet. **Commodore John A. Collins, RAN**, exercised actual control of British naval units in the NEI.

Rear Admiral Doorman was the man charged with executing Helfrich's orders to attack the onrushing Japanese with relentless determination. He was unable to conduct an effective attack at any point during his tenure as commander of the Combined Striking Force. In his final action, he attacked with the determination that Helfrich demanded, but at the cost of his own life and much of the force under his command. (Netherlands Institute for Military History)

OPPOSING FLEETS

IMPERIAL JAPANESE NAVY

The four Mogami-class heavy cruisers of Sentai 7, three of which are shown here in 1938, were the most powerful ships in Vice Admiral Ozawa's Malaya Unit. Of these, *Mogami* and *Mikuma* were active in the battle of the Sunda Strait on March 1, which resulted in the destruction of two Allied cruisers. (US Naval History and Heritage Command)

The primary operational entity of the IJN was the Combined Fleet. In turn, the Combined Fleet was broken down into a number of fleets. The fleets became the basis for major forces allocated operational missions, but the entire structure was very flexible, since ships and divisions could be easily shifted from one fleet to the other to meet operational requirements.

For the NEI campaign, Japanese naval forces were pulled from the Second and Third Fleets. The Second Fleet, also known as the Scouting Force, was based on Hainan Island and was assigned 11 heavy cruisers, including the four Atago-class ships of Sentai 4, three Myoko-class ships of Sentai 5, and all four Mogami-class ships of Sentai 7. Also assigned to the Second Fleet were Destroyer Squadrons 2 and 4. Each of these was assigned a 5,500-ton light cruiser as a flagship, and several divisions of destroyers up to a nominal full strength of 12 ships.

The Third Fleet, based on Formosa, was also known as the Blockade and Transport Force, which well described its wartime missions. Under its direct control was a heavy cruiser, two older light cruisers, and Destroyer Squadron 5 with a light cruiser flagship and two divisions of older destroyers, totaling eight ships. In addition, the First and Second Base Forces were allocated for the conduct of landing operations. Each was comprised of a large number of transports and smaller combatants including patrol boats, minesweepers, minelayers, submarine chasers, and gunboats.

It should be noted that although the attack into Southeast Asia was allocated the majority of the Combined Fleet's combatants, there were other operations which required significant portions of the Combined Fleet. Foremost among these was the Kido Butai which was allocated to the Pearl Harbor operation, and then briefly supported operations in the South Pacific before becoming available to support the NEI campaign in early February. The IJN's battleships were retained in home waters as a strategic reserve, but one section of Sentai 3 with two

One of the IJN's forgotten early-war aircraft was the G3M long-range bomber, later given the Allied reporting name of "Nell". Flying in the absence of Allied fighters, this bomber was very effective, as was shown by its exploits against Force Z, Cavite, and Soerabaja naval bases, and ABDA's Striking Force. (US Naval History and Heritage Command)

Kongo-class fast battleships was allocated to the Southern Expeditionary Force. The rest of the Combined Fleet was occupied supporting the operations in the South and Central Pacific (mainly the Fourth – or Mandate – Fleet), watching the Northern Pacific (the Fifth Fleet). Most of the Combined Fleet's submarines were allocated to support operations against the US Navy as part of the Hawaiian Operation, but 16 older units were allocated to support operations in Southeast Asia.

In all, the Southern Expeditionary Force was allocated two battleships, 12 heavy cruisers, four light cruisers, and some 52 destroyers. On the surface, this was a formidable force, but the pace of operations and the breadth of the operating area meant that it was never concentrated. Imperial Japanese Navy surface units were inadequate to strongly protect all invasion and reinforcement convoys, leaving open the possibility that Allied naval forces could catch a weakly escorted convoy or engage a segment of the Southern Force and defeat it piecemeal.

Vice Admiral Kondo retained direct command of a powerful covering force which included two battleships (*Kongo* and *Haruna*), three heavy cruisers (*Atago*, *Takao*, and *Maya*), and eight destroyers. This force acted in

A small number of B5N1 attack aircraft, like the one shown here in this pre-war photograph, flying from carrier *Ryujo*, played a significant part in the NEI campaign. These aircraft could employ both torpedoes and bombs, but only used bombs during the campaign. They helped repel the Allied Striking Force on February 4 and 15. (US Naval History and Heritage Command)

a distant support role. The direct cover for the many amphibious landings was provided by the two forward groups of the Southern Expeditionary Force. These were the two pincers which led the advance into the NEI. The exact designations of these pincers changed over the course of the campaign, but were most often referred to as the Eastern and Western Forces.

The Eastern Force was under the command of Vice Admiral Takahashi. It was allocated the light carrier *Ryujo*, the four Myoko-class heavy cruisers, Destroyer Squadron 2 with light cruiser *Jintsu* and eight destroyers, and Destroyer Squadron 4 with light cruiser *Naka* and 11 destroyers.

The Western Force, under the command of Vice Admiral Ozawa, was assigned heavy cruiser *Chokai* as his flagship and the four Mogami-class heavy cruisers, and Destroyer Squadron 5 with flagship *Sendai* and seven destroyers.

Imperial Japanese Navy land-based air forces were expected to play a large part in the campaign. The 22nd Air Flotilla, based in French Indochina, was allocated to cover the Malaya operation, and the 21st and 23rd Flotillas were initially allocated to support the attack on the Philippines. All of these were eventually available to support operations against the NEI. These were very powerful offensive forces, as was demonstrated on December 10 when land-based IJN aircraft sank *Prince of Wales* and *Repulse* off Malaya. The aircrews were very highly trained for maritime strike operations and the aircraft they flew were very capable. The mainstay aircraft were the G3M (later given the Allied reporting name of "Nell") and the G4M (later given the reporting name of "Betty"). Both types of aircraft possessed long ranges, and could carry a 1,870-pound Type 91 aerial torpedo or 2,200 pounds of bombs. Against naval targets, they were capable of conducting level bombing, usually from around 10,000ft to avoid most antiaircraft fire, or torpedo bombing. High-level attacks against naval bases were also a priority mission. Both the G3M and G4M were vulnerable to interception by Allied fighter aircraft, but this was not a concern during the campaign.

The ships

Imperial Japanese Navy heavy cruisers were the spearhead of the Japanese naval advance into the NEI. Japanese heavy cruisers were designed to play

Myoko was the first ship in the first class of the IJN's Treaty cruisers. These ships were well over the 10,000-ton treaty limit that assisted Japanese designers in building a balanced ship with immense firepower, high speed, and a significant degree of protection. The Myoko class was superior to US Navy and Royal Navy Treaty cruisers and performed well during the war. (Yamato Museum)

Ashigara, shown here in December 1942 in drydock at the former Royal Navy Seletar Naval Base at Singapore, served as Vice Admiral Takahashi's flagship during the invasion of the Philippines and the NEI. Held in reserve, she did not get an opportunity to engage Allied warships until March 1, when she played a leading role in the destruction of Royal Navy heavy cruiser *Exeter* and destroyer *Encounter*. She remained in NEI waters for most of the remainder of her career and was sunk by the Royal Navy submarine *Trenchant* in the Bangka Strait on June 7, 1945. (Yamato Museum)

several important roles, principally as the centerpieces of night-fighting battle groups. The design of IJN heavy cruisers emphasized firepower, since in order to perform their wartime roles they had to be more heavily armed than comparable US Navy ships and possess the capability to strike at greater ranges than American cruisers. They were capable of conducting long-range gunnery attacks with their 8in. gun batteries. The Myoko class, the first of which was commissioned in 1928, was fitted with a main battery of ten 8in. guns by the time the war began. The next class to commission was the four-ship Atago class, also fitted with ten 8in. guns. The four-ship Mogami class was originally commissioned as light cruisers with 15 6in. guns, but before the start of the war was upgraded to a main battery of ten 8in. guns. The maximum range of the 8in. guns fitted to these three classes ranged between 31,606 and 32,153 yards. The Japanese believed that the fire-control equipment fitted to their cruisers gave their 8in. guns an effective engagement range of 21,873 yards, but they often engaged targets at even longer ranges. However, at extended ranges the twin-gun 8in. turret suffered from significant dispersion problems which affected accuracy.

Additionally, IJN heavy cruisers were fitted with a heavy torpedo battery. At the start of the Pacific War, Myoko-class units carried 16 torpedo tubes and 18 reload torpedoes. This was matched by two ships in the Atago class, but the Mogami class carried only 12 torpedo tubes with reloads. Beginning in 1938, Japanese heavy cruisers were provided with a top secret new torpedo – the Type 93 Model 1 Modification 2. This was a formidable weapon, vastly superior to any Allied torpedo. It carried a 1,082-pound warhead, was wakeless since it was oxygen propelled, and had a range up to 43,746 yards at 36 knots. Carrying such powerful weapons greatly enhanced the firepower of IJN heavy cruisers, but there was a potential downside. Carrying such weapons presented a real danger if the unprotected warheads were hit during the combat. This occurred aboard IJN heavy cruisers several times during the war and the results were devastating.

Imperial Japanese Navy light cruisers were less formidable, since their primary mission was to act as flagships for destroyer squadrons. The IJN commissioned 14 5,500-ton light cruisers between 1920 and 1925. These were fitted with seven 5.5in. single mounts at the start of the war. All carried torpedo mounts, but only those actually assigned as destroyer squadron flagships were equipped with the Type 93 torpedo. These ships included all three Sendai class, two of which, *Naka* and *Jintsu*, were active in the NEI campaign.

Just as Japanese heavy cruisers were designed to be larger and more powerfully armed than their Allied counterparts, the same held true for the IJN's destroyers. Japanese destroyers were maximized for offensive punch against surface ships; they were superb torpedo boats but were not well-rounded platforms for antiair and antisubmarine combat. In the NEI campaign, these weaknesses did not matter. Beginning with the Special Type destroyer (also known as the Fubuki class), IJN destroyers set the pace with a combination of high speed and heavy armament. Fubuki-class ships carried six 5in. guns and nine torpedoes with three reloads. The next class of destroyers, the six-ship Hatsuhara class, carried five 5in. guns and six torpedo tubes with six reloads. The Shiratsuyu class introduced the quadruple torpedo mount; this class was fitted with five 5in. guns and eight torpedo tubes with another eight reloads. The ten-ship Asashio class played a prominent role in the NEI campaign. These ships had a top speed of 35 knots and were armed with six 5in. guns in three dual mounts. Each ship carried eight torpedo types and another eight reloads. The follow-on to the Asashio class was the Kagero class, several of which were active in the NEI campaign. This class had similar capabilities to the Asashio class. A division of the older Kamikaze class also saw action during the NEI campaign. These ships, dating from 1922, carried four 4.7in. guns and six 21in. (compared to the 24in. tubes in the classes already discussed) torpedo tubes with no reloads.

Training

Imperial Japanese Navy training was extremely intense and was meant to simulate actual battle conditions. The seriousness of such rigorous training was displayed in 1927 when during a night torpedo exercise a destroyer was sunk in a collision with the loss of 104 men, another destroyer was heavily

Jintsu was one of the IJN's most successful light cruisers during the war. She was used in her intended role as the leader of a destroyer squadron during the NEI campaign and then later at Midway and throughout the Guadalcanal campaign, until being sunk by US Navy cruiser gunfire in the battle of Kolombangara in July 1943 in the central Solomons. (Yamato Museum)

damaged with 29 more casualties, and two cruisers were also damaged. The pace of training was relentless, especially when the training year culminated in October. Imperial Japanese Navy officers described the training as tougher than actual combat. The result was a finely honed instrument by the beginning of the war.

Night combat capabilities and doctrine

Night combat was an area of special emphasis in IJN pre-war training. Night combat was a central tenet of Japanese naval doctrine, since it was the primary method by which highly trained IJN ships could turn the tables on the larger US Navy. Night combat tactics were re-worked after the Type 93 torpedo entered service, beginning in 1936. To use the long range of this weapon, the heavy cruisers were trained to fire them at long range in day or night combat. This "long-distance concealed firing" was expected to cripple the enemy before he knew he was in danger. When the IJN's destroyers received the Type 93, and not all did before the start of the war, their tactics were similar. The Japanese constantly rehearsed torpedo tactics, and quick reloading of torpedo tubes was a key skill. A well-drilled crew could accomplish this in 15 minutes. This allowed Japanese cruisers and destroyers to fire a salvo of torpedoes, disengage to reload, and then fire a second salvo.

Night combat was more than just well-rehearsed torpedo tactics. The Japanese practiced using large searchlights to illuminate targets. Star shells and flares deployed by cruiser floatplanes were also developed. Another key Japanese advantage was their superior optical equipment, which was critical in the era before radar.

The IJN placed great importance on its top-secret long-range torpedo at the start of the Pacific War. It devised tactics to utilize the capabilities of these weapons which gave the Japanese the ability to inflict stand-off blows against Allied surface ships. During the NEI campaign, the performance of this wonder weapon was disappointing, since only three hit out of the large numbers that were expended. (Author's Collection)

ALLIED NAVAL FORCES

Allied naval forces committed to the defense of the NEI were inadequate for the task. Simply put, the IJN operated more powerful ships manned by better-trained crews and had the massive advantage of operating with a powerful naval air arm. Allied naval forces operated throughout the campaign with significant handicaps including a confusing command situation, lack of fighter cover, and lack of air reconnaissance. During the campaign, Allied naval forces were subjected to increasing strain. Logistics support broke down, limiting supplies of fuel and ammunition. Communications were a constant problem, since four different navies were present. The Allies did not possess a set of mutually intelligible codes for even basic maneuvers, which was a constant headache for Doorman when he devised his cruising dispositions and maneuvered his force. Doorman issued orders in Dutch, and these were transmitted by Allied liaison and communication personnel aboard his flagship to the other ships in the force. The force did not share a common set of tactics, forcing Doorman to resort to a basic battle plan.

Sealion photographed in October 1939 running trials. She was the first US Navy submarine lost during the war, when she was bombed at Cavite Navy Yard in the Philippines on December 10. (US Naval History and Heritage Command)

Houston was a Northampton-class heavy cruiser which was commissioned in 1930. Note the ship's two large masts, the three 8in. triple turrets (two forward and one aft), and the aviation facilities between the two stacks. Compared to IJN heavy cruisers, she was under-armed and under protected. (US Naval History and Heritage Command)

The Asiatic Fleet

The US Navy's standing Western Pacific force was weak, and it received no reinforcements during the campaign. With few exceptions, it was built around expendable ships. Its centerpiece was three cruisers and 13 destroyers. The only real source of potential strength was the fleet's 29 submarines. However, their crews lacked experience and spent the months leading up to the war exercising exceedingly conservative tactics. These called for boats to execute torpedo attacks while submerged to as much as 100 feet using only sound bearings. Commanding officers were not allowed to make attacks at periscope depth or to expose their periscopes. There was also the issue of defective torpedoes, which further lessened their effectiveness. The most crippling factor was the lack of aggression among the commanding officers. Combined with tactics which emphasized stealth over attack, it made the submarines a non-factor in the campaign.

Heavy cruiser Houston was the flagship of the fleet. She was commissioned in 1930 and was one of the US Navy's first generation "Treaty" cruisers, which carried a strong main battery (nine 8in. guns) but were under-protected compared to IJN heavy cruisers. The ship carried a strong antiaircraft battery of eight 5in./25 guns, along with four newly installed quad 1.1in. mounts. US Navy heavy cruisers did not carry torpedoes. Early in February, Houston suffered damage which disabled

Light cruiser *Boise* photographed in early November 1941 off Hawaii in a Measure 1 camouflage scheme. Note the heavy main armament of 15 6in. guns in five triple turrets. She was among the most powerful light cruisers in the world in early 1942, and possessed fighting power and protection equal to IJN heavy cruisers. Forced out of the NEI campaign after being grounded on an uncharted reef, the ship returned to service in time for the Guadalcanal campaign, where she was damaged in October at the battle of Cape Esperance. After being repaired again, she participated in the invasions of Sicily and Salerno in the Mediterranean. Returning to the Pacific in late 1943, her last major operation was the invasion of Borneo in 1945. (US Naval History and Heritage Command)

her aft 8in. turret and was forced to fight the remainder of the campaign without it. Two light cruisers were also assigned to the fleet. *Boise* was a Brooklyn-class cruiser and was the fleet's most modern asset. At 12,207 tons full load, she was larger than most Treaty heavy cruisers. Her main battery consisted of 15 6in. guns; each of which could fire up to ten rounds per minute. She was well protected and carried a comparable antiaircraft fit to *Houston*. *Marblehead* was an Omaha-class light cruiser. Commissioned in 1924, her weak protection and the antiquated main battery layout of her ten 6in. single guns made her unsuitable for front-line duties, hence her assignment to the Asiatic Fleet.

The fleet's destroyers all dated from the US Navy's World War I building program. The 1,200-ton full-load ships were commissioned with four 4in./50 guns and 12 21in. torpedo tubes. US Navy destroyer torpedoes were the Mark 8. They suffered from reliability issues and had a maximum range of 16,000 yards at 26 knots. By the start of the Pacific War, these ships retained the same armament with only the addition of a totally inadequate single 3in. gun and three to four .50-cal. machine guns for antiaircraft protection. Capable of 33–34 knots when commissioned, by 1941 they could

Light cruiser *Marblehead*, shown here in this pre-war photograph, was assigned to the Asiatic Fleet at the start of the war. Note the archaic arrangement of the forward 6in. guns with a twin turret and four in awkward casemate arrangements. Designed for scouting, the Omaha-class light cruisers were cramped, poorly protected, and were considered second-rate by the start of the Pacific War. Repaired following damage in February 1942, *Marblehead* operated primarily in the South Atlantic for the remainder of the war, looking for Axis blockade runners. (US Naval History and Heritage Command)

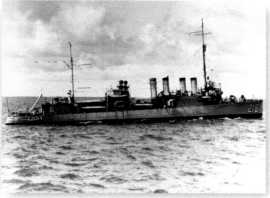

barely make 28–30 knots. By the end of the campaign, torpedoes were in increasingly short supply. At Java Sea, some destroyers carried as few as six.

The entire fleet was poorly trained in the types of operations they most likely would be expected to perform. For example, the destroyers did not practice night fighting. Other exercises were brief and unrealistic, mainly due to budgetary reasons. Maintenance was also a real issue, due to the advanced age of almost all ships in the fleet and because spare parts were unavailable.

The entire air component of the Asiatic Fleet was comprised of Patrol Wing 10 with its 28 PBY-4 Catalina flying boats. These were excellent at performing reconnaissance but possessed very limited strike capabilities. Of note, the Asiatic Fleet was totally dependent on other services or nations for air defense.

The Royal Navy

The ships that the Royal Navy committed to the defense of the NEI were also largely second rate. They were led by the heavy cruiser *Exeter*, which was the hero of the December 1939 engagement with the German armored ship *Graf Spee* at the battle of the River Plate. Damaged during the engagement, she was repaired and modernized over the following year. Of the Royal Navy's 15 heavy cruisers, *Exeter* and her sister ship *York* were the smallest (just over 10,000 tons full load) and only carried six 8in. guns instead of the usual eight. She did carry six torpedo tubes, but was relatively lightly armored with

The sister ship of *Perth* was *Hobart*, also a modified Leander-class light cruiser, which was transferred to the Royal Australian Navy in 1938. In the final stages of the campaign, she was assigned to the Western Striking Force and thus saw no action against the Japanese surface forces which ensured her survival beyond the fall of the NEI. (US Naval History and Heritage Command)

a main belt of 3in. During her modernization, she received early warning and fire-control radars, making her the only radar-equipped ship in the campaign.

The British naval contingent included several light cruisers. The best were two modified Leander-class light cruisers, *Hobart* and *Perth*, which were transferred to the Royal Australian Navy in 1938 and 1939, respectively. Both were veteran ships, with *Perth* in particular establishing a fine war record in the Mediterranean from 1940 to 1941. Both ships carried eight 6in. guns and eight 21in. torpedo tubes, but were poorly protected. Two D-class cruisers, *Dragon* and *Danae*, were also available, but dated from 1918 and were unsuited for front-line duties. Both carried six 6in. guns in single mounts and 12 21in. torpedo tubes.

The small number of British destroyers available was a mixed lot. Three E-class ships were commissioned in 1934. *Electra* and *Express* came to the Far East as escorts for *Prince of Wales* and *Encounter* was detached from the Mediterranean Fleet. These ships displaced around 1,500 tons, making them smaller than all modern Japanese destroyers. Each carried four single 4.7in. guns and eight 21in. torpedo tubes and all were veteran ships. *Electra* survived the campaign because she was damaged when she was rescuing survivors from *Prince of Wales* on December 10 and was forced to leave the area and go to Ceylon during the first part of February.

Perth was originally commissioned as HMS *Amphion* in 1936 and transferred to the Royal Australian Navy in 1939. Armed with eight 6in. guns, eight 4in. guns, and eight 21in. torpedo tubes, *Perth* was a balanced cruiser design which had an active and fine war record in the Mediterranean Sea earlier in the war. Superior to Japanese light cruisers, she was overwhelmed at the battle of the Sunda Strait. In 2013, it was revealed that the wreck had been stripped of many of its parts with scrappers using explosives to break up the ship. (US Naval History and Heritage Command)

This is D-class light cruiser *Danae* photographed before the war. Note the individual 6in. gun mounts and two port-side triple torpedo mounts. Commissioned in 1918, *Danae* was obsolescent by the start of the Pacific War. Assigned to convoy escort duty and then the Western Striking Force, the two D-class cruisers never had a chance to engage the Japanese. (US Naval History and Heritage Command)

Jupiter, also detached from the Mediterranean Fleet, was commissioned in 1939 and possessed a heavier armament of three twin 4.7in. mounts and ten 21in. torpedoes in quintuple mounts. She had already bloodied the Japanese by sinking submarine *I-60* on January 17, 1942. In addition, several 1,220-ton full load S-class destroyers were assigned to the Eastern Fleet. Commissioned between 1918 and 1919, they carried three 4in. guns and four torpedo tubes. The principal British destroyer torpedo at this point of the war was the Mark IX, with a maximum range of 15,000 yards at 35 knots.

The Royal Netherlands Navy

Dutch naval forces in the NEI were not prepared for the start of the war. Three cruisers were in commission, but all were outclassed by their

De Ruyter was the most powerful unit in the RNN's East Indies Squadron but was a thoroughly inferior light cruiser design in terms of firepower, protection, and speed. Two of the ship's twin 5.9in. turrets can be seen in this view; in total, seven 5.9in. guns were carried. No heavy antiaircraft guns were carried; the cluster of five twin 40mm mounts can be seen forward of the twin 6in. turrets. No torpedoes were carried. The main belt was only fitted with two inches of armor. Maximum speed was a mediocre 32 knots. When matched against Japanese heavy cruisers, the result was predictable. (Netherlands Institute for Military History)

foreign counterparts. The most modern ship, *De Ruyter*, was launched in 1935 and armed with seven 5.9in. guns. She carried no torpedoes, had an inadequate antiaircraft battery and was lightly armored. *Java*, launched in 1921, was based on the design of German World War I cruisers and carried a main battery of ten 5.9in. guns, all single mounts, of which only seven could be fired broadside. *Tromp* was only 4,215 tons full load, indicating she was designed as a destroyer flotilla leader; she carried a main battery of six 5.9in. guns in twin turrets. In addition to the cruisers, the Dutch had seven destroyers in commission. They were all of the same class, based on a British design, and were constructed in the Netherlands beginning in 1925. Each carried four 4.7in. guns in single mounts and six torpedo tubes. The standard Dutch torpedo was

Dutch light cruiser *Java* shown in this pre-war photograph. Her design was based on World War I German light cruisers, as is evident in this view. Note the individual 5.9in. gun mounts. (Netherlands Institute for Military History)

TROMP
Netherlands - CL
(TROMP Class)
1938

Tromp was originally authorized as a destroyer flotilla leader in 1931 but was completed as a small light cruiser. The ship was relatively heavily armed with six 5.9in. guns and six 21in. torpedo tubes on a standard displacement of only 3,450 tons. She survived the war and was present at the Japanese surrender in the NEI in September 1945. (US Naval History and Heritage Command)

a 21in. British-built weapon with a maximum range of 10,936 yards at 28 knots. The Dutch also operated 15 submarines in the NEI. Most were dated designs from the 1920s. All of the Dutch naval units suffered from maintenance and personnel problems, since parts could not be acquired from the Netherlands and repair facilities in the NEI were inadequate to keep the fleet ready. One destroyer, *Witte de With*, lacked a crew. When *Van Ghent* ran aground and was scuttled, her entire crew was moved to *Witte de With*, but the destroyer was not available until February 22. In general, Dutch training was not robust, but they did emphasize night combat. No Dutch ship carried radar.

Dutch naval bases on Java were the primary facilities used by Allied naval forces during the campaign. The primary base was at Soerabaja, which was located on Java's northeast coast. It had modern facilities including a 15,000-ton drydock. Tandjong Priok, the port for Batavia, was located on northwest Java. This was a commercial port, not a naval base. The only base on Java's southern coast was Tjilatjap, which became increasingly important during the campaign for funneling reinforcements into Java. The port contained few facilities, but in December the Dutch moved an 8,000-ton floating drydock there to at least provide some repair capability. None of these bases possessed adequate air defenses.

ORDERS OF BATTLE

BATTLE OF BALIKPAPAN

United States Navy (US Navy)
Destroyer Division 5 (Commander Paul Talbot)
    Destroyers *John D. Ford* (flagship), *Parrott, Paul Jones, Pope*

Imperial Japanese Navy
Elements of Base Force 2 (Rear Admiral Nishimura Shoji)
Patrol Boats *P-36, P-37, P-38*
Minesweepers *W-15, W-16, W-17, W-18*
Submarine Chasers *Ch-10, Ch-11, Ch-12*

BATTLE OF BADOENG STRAIT

ABDA Naval Forces
First Striking Force (Rear Admiral Karel Doorman, Royal Netherlands
    Navy (RNN))
Light Cruisers *De Ruyter* (flagship), *Java* (RNN)
Destroyers *Piet Hein* (RNN), *John D. Ford, Pope* (US Navy)

Second Striking Force (Captain J. B. de Meester, RNN)
Light Cruiser *Tromp* (RNN)
Destroyer Division 58 (Commander Thomas Binford, US Navy)
    Destroyers *Stewart* (flagship), *John D. Edwards, Parrott, Pillsbury*

Third Striking Force
Torpedo Boats – 8 (RNN)

Imperial Japanese Navy
Destroyer Division 8 (Captain Abe Toshio)
    Destroyers *Ooshio* (flagship), *Asashio, Arashio, Michishio*

BATTLE OF THE JAVA SEA

ABDA Naval Forces
Combined Striking Force (Rear Admiral Karel Doorman, RNN)
Heavy Cruisers *Exeter* (Royal Navy (RN)), *Houston* (US Navy)
Light Cruisers *De Ruyter* (flagship), *Java* (RNN), *Perth* (Royal Australian
    Navy (RAN))
Destroyers *Witte de With, Kortenaer* (RNN), *Electra, Encounter, Jupiter*
    (RN)
Destroyer Division 58 (Commander Binford, US Navy)
    Destroyers *John D. Edwards* (flagship), *Alden, John D. Ford,*
    Paul Jones

Imperial Japanese Navy
Sentai 5 (Rear Admiral Takagi Takeo)
Heavy Cruisers *Nachi* (flagship), *Haguro*
Destroyer Squadron 2 (Rear Admiral Tanaka Razio)
    Light Cruiser *Jintsu* (flagship)
    Destroyer Division 7 (Captain Konishi Kaname)
    Destroyers *Sazanami, Ushio*
    Destroyer Division 16 (Captain Shibuya Shiro)
    Destroyers *Amatsukaze, Hatsukaze, Tokitsukaze, Yukikaze*
    Destroyer Division 24
    Destroyers *Kawakaze, Yamakaze*
Destroyer Squadron 4 (Rear Admiral Nishimura Shoji)
    Light Cruiser *Naka* (flagship)
    Destroyer Division 2 (Captain Tachibana Masao)
    Destroyers *Harusame, Murasame, Samidare, Yudachi*
    Destroyer Division 9 (Captain Sato Yasuo)
    Destroyers *Asagumo, Minegumo*

BATTLE OF THE SUNDA STRAIT

Allied Naval Forces (Captain H. Walker, RN)
Heavy Cruiser *Houston* (US Navy)
Light Cruiser *Perth* (RAN)
Destroyer *Evertsen* (RNN)

Imperial Japanese Navy (Rear Admiral Hara Kenzaburo)
Sentai 7, Section 2 (Captain Sakiyama Shakao)
    Heavy Cruisers *Mogami* (flagship), *Mikuma*
Destroyer Squadron 2 (Rear Admiral Hara Kenzaburo)
    Light Cruiser *Natori* (flagship)
    Destroyer Division 5 (Captain Nomaguchi, Kanetomo)
    Destroyers *Harukaze* (flagship), *Hatakaze, Asakaze*
    Destroyer Division 11 (Captain Shoji Kiichiro)
    Destroyers *Shirayuki* (flagship), *Fubuki, Hatsuyuki*
    Destroyer Division 12 (Captain Ogawa Nobuki)
    Destroyers *Shirakumo* (flagship), *Murakumo*

SECOND BATTLE OF THE JAVA SEA

Allied Naval Forces (Captain O. L. Gordon, RN)
Heavy Cruiser *Exeter* (RN)
Destroyers *Encounter* (US Navy), *Pope* (US Navy)

Imperial Japanese Navy (Vice Admiral Takahashi Ibo)
Support Force (Vice Admiral Takahashi Ibo)
Heavy Cruisers *Ashigara* (flagship), *Myoko*
Destroyers *Akebono, Ikazuchi*
Sentai 5 (Rear Admiral Takagi Takeo)
    Heavy Cruisers *Nachi* (flagship), *Haguro*
    Destroyer Division 24
    Destroyers *Kawakaze, Yamakaze*

OPPOSING PLANS

THE JAPANESE PLAN

The most important aspect of Japan's war plans for the initial phase of the war was the seizure of the resources of Southeast Asia. The Japanese had to quickly gain and bring back into operation the oil fields of Borneo, Java, and Sumatra. Of these, the Sumatran wells were the most important. The principal Allied military, air, and naval forces in Southeast Asia were the British garrison in Malaya. These had to be neutralized concurrent with the drive into the NEI. Furthermore, the Japanese faced the strategic imperative to neutralize American forces in the Philippines, since they were convinced that the United States would intervene if Japan attacked British and Dutch possessions in Southeast Asia. Added to the difficulty for the Japanese that the campaign against British, American, and Dutch forces was the requirement to move as quickly as possible before the Dutch had the opportunity to destroy the economic facilities and before the British and Americans could reinforce their possessions.

The forces available to the Japanese were barely sufficient for the expansive operation they were embarking on. The lack of shipping to transport the invasion forces meant that the operations would have to be conducted in sequence. In five months, the Japanese envisioned completing the three phases of the campaign to bring Southeast Asia under their control. In the first phase, the forward outposts of the Allied defenses were slated for occupation. These included Hong Kong, northern Malaya, British Borneo, Sarawak, and the Philippines. The second phase required the occupation of the entire Malay Peninsula, including Singapore, and the northern islands of the NEI. Finally, in the third phase, Sumatra and Java were to be occupied.

The key to the Japanese plan was maintaining a relentless pace. The Japanese plan was almost reckless, but as a planning assumption they made the assessment that the Allies would be unable to offer an adequate defense. Despite the bravery of the Allied forces, the initial Japanese assessment proved correct and the Japanese were able to execute their bold plan on time and with marginal losses. Another key was the early seizure of air superiority and the imperative that advances only be conducted under friendly air protection. The Japanese planned to seize an airfield and move south under the protection of the aircraft moved to occupy the just-captured facility and then repeat the procedure. Since all the IJN's fleet carriers were initially supporting the Hawaiian Operation, the burden for supporting the invasion of the NEI was placed on the land-based 11th Air Fleet with its three air flotillas. The Japanese made good use of the light carrier *Ryujo* and a number of seaplane carriers to provide local air cover, but the entire plan was dependent on land-based air forces gaining air superiority over the next objective.

The maneuver scheme for the principal naval forces was simple. Vice Admiral Kondo would provide distant support for the invasion forces with his heavy force built around two battleships. The Eastern Force, under Vice Admiral Takahashi, was initially based at Palau. After supporting the occupation of Mindanao in the Philippines, it would support the occupation of Jolo, Tarakan, Balikpapen, and Banjermasin on eastern and southern Borneo; then Menado, Makassar, and Kendari in the Celebeas; then Ambon in the Moluccas; then Timor in the Lesser Soendas. The final objective was the occupation of Java, for which the Eastern and Western Forces would unite. Before reaching Java, the Western Force, under Vice Admiral Ozawa, was initially based out of Hainan Island and Cam Ranh Bay in French Indochina. This force was initially focused on protecting the landings in southern Thailand and northern Malaya. After these, Borneo was next, followed by points on Sumatra, principally the oil fields at Palembang. The final seizure of Java would mark the end of the campaign.

THE ALLIED PLAN

Before the war, the Allies to be did not possess coherent plans on how to deal with Japanese aggression. British defense planning to defend their Far East possessions centered on the major naval base at Singapore. As impressive as this base was when it was completed, it lacked a fleet. The Royal Navy simply lacked the means to assemble a fleet for duty in the Far East as the war raged in Europe. Reflecting this reality, London admitted to its military command in Malaya in September 1939 that it could be as long as six months before a fleet could be assembled and sent east. In late 1941, as Great Britain's war fortunes in Europe were at low ebb, it became apparent that it was impossible for the Royal Navy to shift a significant force to the Far East. The lack of a naval force to protect or relieve Singapore meant that it had to be held by ground and air forces, but in both these areas the British forces in Malaya were greatly inadequate. The bottom line was that British naval forces were inadequate to defend Singapore, much less to provide assistance to the Dutch.

Dutch defense strategy was clearly dependent upon intervention by the British or Americans, or both, to defend the NEI. In spite of this obvious circumstance, the Dutch refused to conduct joint defense planning with their prospective allies before the war. With a small naval force, supported by a small air force of some 200 combat aircraft, and with an under-equipped and poorly trained ground force of only three divisions, the NEI was virtually undefended. Since the Netherlands were occupied by the Germans, there was no source of potential reinforcement for the NEI, and keeping the ships and aircraft already deployed to the NEI operational was increasingly difficult.

The only power with the potential capability to defend the NEI was the United States. However, the focus of American defense planning in the Far East was the defense of the Philippines, then an American possession. The

US Navy had a permanent presence in the region, a small force given the grandiloquent name of the Asiatic Fleet. The Asiatic Fleet was unclear as to its commitments in the period immediately before the war. Pre-war plans recognized that the Philippines could not be defended and that no major attempt by the Pacific Fleet to relief the garrison there should be attempted. This left the Asiatic Fleet on its own. It was tasked with buying time in the defense of the Philippines, and when this became impossible, to withdraw southward and support the British defense of Malaya or the defense of the NEI.

When war was imminent, it was confirmed that no naval reinforcements for Southeast Asia were forthcoming from the US Navy's Pacific Fleet. The Royal Navy was able to send a small deterrent force to the Far East in the form of Force Z. This made preservation of Singapore an Allied, not just a British, imperative. It was also soon clear that no naval defense could be mounted of the Philippines because of its exposed position. In the days before the war, Hart pulled his forces off their China stations and from the main naval base at Cavite in Manila Bay, and moved his forces south for preservation. For the Asiatic Fleet, force preservation from the initial Japanese onslaught was key. Once ejected from its main base in Manila Bay, the Asiatic Fleet was ordered to head south and operate out of bases in the NEI and Darwin in northwest Australia. Combined with the Dutch, and whatever British units were left after the Force Z debacle, an Allied striking force could be formed to mount a defense of the NEI. The overriding Allied strategy was to defend the Malay Barrier and keep the Japanese out of the Indian Ocean. The Japanese invasion showed how fragile any Allied plans were.

THE CAMPAIGN

With the rout of British forces on Malaya well underway, and the withdrawal of American forces into the Bataan Peninsula, the battle for the NEI was about to begin. Admiral Hart moved to Java by submarine and arrived safely there on January 1, 1942. Upon his arrival, he learned he had been named commander of ABDA naval forces. He was immediately faced with the political intrigues of the Dutch authorities on Java and the approaching Japanese storm.

THE BATTLE OF BALIKPAPAN

The Japanese campaign to conquer the NEI began on December 25, 1941 with a landing on Jolo Island in the Sulu Archipelago. The next move was conducted by the Eastern Force on January 11 when Special Naval Landing Force (SNLF) troops landed at Menado and Kema on the northern Celebes, supported by SNLF paratroopers. The important port of Kendari was located further south on Celebes. Hart assessed that this was the next Japanese target and made plans to intercept a Japanese thrust in that direction. Until now, American naval forces had not engaged the Japanese and Hart thought it was past time to do so. While British and Dutch naval forces were primarily occupied in escorting convoys, the first significant naval action of the campaign would be initiated by the Americans.

The pace of the Japanese advance increased when on January 12 an invasion force under Rear Admiral Nishimura captured Tarakan on northeast Borneo. The Dutch defense was weak, and the Japanese captured the airfield intact. The airfield was brought into operation within days, which provided air cover for the next operation. This was a landing on Balikpapan which was an important port and oil facility on Borneo's southeast coast. Nishimura sortied on January 21 with an invasion force for Balikpapan.

In response to the Japanese advances on Borneo and in the Celebes, Rear Admiral Glassford was ordered to bring Task Force 5, the Asiatic Fleet's striking force, to readiness. At various times, the force included cruisers *Houston*, *Boise*, *Marblehead*, and as many as eight destroyers. On January 17, Glassford led the cruisers, escorted by six destroyers, to attack a Japanese force reported off Kema. On this occasion, as on many, the intelligence was faulty. Three days later, in response to Dutch reports of Japanese activity in the Makassar Strait, Glassford departed Koepang on Timor Island with

Battle of Balikpapan, January 24, 1942

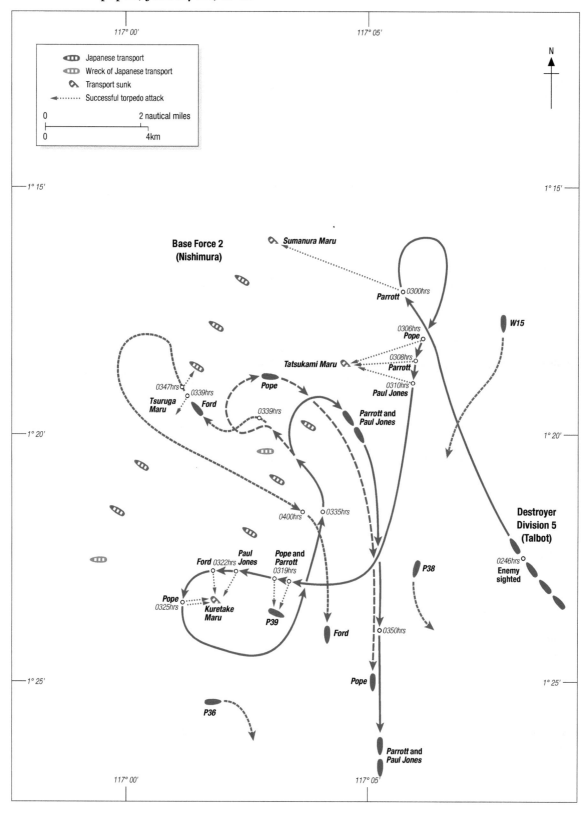

USS FORD. GR 10313.

Boise and *Marblehead* escorted by six destroyers. While transiting, disaster struck. *Boise*, the most powerful unit in the Asiatic Fleet, struck an uncharted reef in the Sape Strait on January 21. The cruiser suffered a 120ft-long gash to her hull which caused flooding damage to some of her machinery. *Boise* was forced to leave the area for repairs, a major loss for the Americans but almost certainly a fortuitous event for the ship and its crew. The latest report of Japanese activity was also false, but as a precaution, Glassford ordered the four destroyers of Destroyer Division 59 to patrol in the southern Makassar Strait.

The continued advance of the Japanese Eastern Force and Hart's prodding to Glassford to engage the Japanese made a naval clash inevitable. On January 22, an American flying boat sighted a large Japanese convoy under heavy escort heading toward Balikpapan. Again, Hart ordered Task Force 5 to engage. By now, *Houston* and two destroyers had resumed escort duties, the damaged *Boise* was headed out of the area, and *Marblehead* was dealing with a turbine problem which limited her to 15 knots. Instead of Task Force 5's original and powerful composition of three cruisers and eight destroyers, the nearest American units were the four destroyers of Division 5 under Commander Paul H. Talbot. These moved north, beginning on the morning of January 23. The weather and seas during the day were bad, which allowed the Americans to make their approach undetected. Talbot intended to mount a surprise attack on the anchored Japanese invasion force two hours before dawn. He ordered his destroyers to use their torpedoes first; when these were expended, then gunfire. *Marblehead* and one destroyer were ordered north to cover the withdrawal of the destroyers.

The US Navy's flush deck destroyers were bad sea boats, since they had narrow hulls and were top heavy and prone to rolling. Of their four 4in. guns, only three could be fired broadside. On the positive side, the ships did carry a heavy torpedo battery of 12 tubes, which reflected a design emphasis on producing a good torpedo boat. This is a photograph of *John D. Ford* soon after her completion. (US Naval History and Heritage Command)

Sailors work on one of the triple torpedo launchers in a flush-deck destroyer in this pre-war photograph. These launchers fired the Mark 8 torpedo, which dated from World War I and was standard issue on flush-deck destroyers at the start of the war. It was riddled with reliability problems, like running too deep and failing to explode when it hit a target. This made any success by the Asiatic Fleet's destroyers remarkable, like the raid at Balikpapan when five Japanese ships were sunk despite having to use this weapon. (US Naval History and Heritage Command)

Awaiting the four American destroyers was a much more powerful force under Nishimura. The invasion force was embarked on 15 transports and escorted by Destroyer Squadron 4 with light cruiser *Naka* and ten destroyers. Providing close-in escort were three patrol boats (ex-Momi-class destroyers with their torpedo tubes removed but still fitted with two 4.7in. guns), four minesweepers (each with two 4.7in. guns), and three subchasers. During the evening of January 24, one of the transports was hit by Dutch aircraft and later abandoned. The remaining 14 transports arrived off Balikpapan at 2015hrs and anchored in two rows. Just before midnight, a Dutch submarine launched four torpedoes at *Naka*; these missed their target but hit another of the transports. As the American destroyers neared their target, Nishimura deployed *Naka* and his destroyers west of the convoy, the three patrol boats to the south, and the four minesweepers to the north.

The American destroyers swept into the anchorage at 27 knots. The anchored transports were silhouetted by the fires from the oil facilities ashore which had been set afire by the Dutch. Several Japanese ships spotted the American destroyers, but none raised a proper alarm. In the minutes before 0300hrs, minesweeper *W15* spotted the approaching Americans. At first they were taken for *Naka*, which also had four stacks. Before the Japanese ship could engage, the four destroyers disappeared into the night. The Americans identified the minesweeper as a destroyer and three of the destroyers fired a total of seven torpedoes at the ship, but the angle was unfavorable and none hit.

Talbot ordered his four destroyers to come around for another slashing attack against the anchored convoy. As this maneuver was taking place, *Parrott* fired three torpedoes at the northernmost transport in the line closest to shore. At least one hit the *Sumanura Maru*, which was carrying ammunition. The resulting explosion accounted for the transport and all but nine of her crew.

As Talbot's force was steering south, both *John D. Ford* and *Pope* fired a torpedo at patrol boat *P38*. Minutes later at 0306hrs, *Pope* spotted a group of ships and fired five torpedoes, followed by *Parrott* and *Paul Jones* firing one each. These accounted for transport *Tatsukami Maru*. At 0314hrs, the American column turned to starboard to attack the southern part of the anchorage. *John D. Ford* fired a torpedo at a target to port identified as a destroyer; this was followed at 0319hrs by *Pope* firing five and *Parrott* three torpedoes at another "destroyer" to port. Three of these eight fish hit the 985-ton *P37* and she sank with the loss of 35 men. *Paul Jones* fired two torpedoes at the nearby *Kuretake Maru*, and the second one hit its target at 0325hrs.

Talbot continued his rampage inside the anchorage, even though two of his destroyers were out of torpedoes. *Pope* and *Parrott* now used their 4in. guns and claimed multiple hits on transports and "destroyers." Up until this point, the American column maintained its cohesion, making targeting easier in the smoke and confusion. At 0340hrs, however, Talbot's flagship *John D. Ford* lost contact with the other three destroyers, which headed south out of the action. *John D. Ford* still had torpedoes, and fired her last two at *Tsuruga Maru* at 0346hrs. This was the transport hit four hours earlier by the Dutch submarine; the American torpedoes finished her off. *John D. Ford* then proceeded to pummel two more transports with 4in. gunfire at close range. Though damaged, neither sank. By 0410hrs, *John D. Ford* was also headed south. The only damage to the American force was a small-caliber hit on *John D. Ford*, which wounded four men.

The American attack had been bold and resulted in a brilliant tactical victory. Even using their unreliable torpedoes, the final tally was four transports and a patrol boat sunk. By any measure, this was a successful action. The Japanese response was totally ineffective despite their prowess at night combat. Nishimura underestimated the Americans and for some reason did not believe more than a single enemy destroyer could penetrate the anchorage. He was more concerned about possible submarine and torpedo boat attacks and in the early minutes of the battle was on *Naka* some seven miles northeast of the anchored convoy. Even as the battle was drawing to a close, Nishimura was still over three miles east of the convoy. More concerned about a submarine attack, he left his convoy to the mercy of the American destroyers.

Victory at Balikpapan did not stop or even delay the Japanese advance. On January 24, Kendari in the Celebes was captured with its fine port and well-equipped airfield complex. From here, the naval base at Soerabaja was within range of Japanese bombers. The first raid on the base occurred on February 3 and continued on a virtually daily basis until the end of the campaign.

THE ABDA STRIKING FORCE IS FORMED

Hart established the ABDA Striking Force on February 1. Initially, it was comprised only of available American and Dutch warships. The following day, he selected the Striking Force's commander – Dutch Rear Admiral

Karel Doorman. By February 3, the Combined Striking Force was gathered east of Soerabaja. Present was *Houston*, *Marblehead*, and seven American destroyers. They were joined for the first time by Dutch cruisers *De Ruyter* and *Tromp*, with three more Dutch destroyers on their way. Hart was determined to use this powerful force to attack the Japanese invasion force headed for Makassar on the southern Celebes. In discussion with Doorman, they decided to sortie the Striking Force at midnight on February 4 and head through the Flores Sea toward Makassar. This plan presented the possibility of attacking the Japanese, but to do so they had to transit through the Flores Sea in daylight. Furthermore, the Japanese air strike on Soerabaja on February 3 had sighted the Striking Force in its nearby anchorage. This meant the potential for surprise had been eliminated.

The weight of Japanese air power made itself felt on February 4. After the detachment of three American destroyers to escort oiler *Pecos* and the addition of the three Dutch destroyers, the Combined Striking Force totaled the four cruisers and seven destroyers (four American and three Dutch). This force departed Soerabaja and transited to the east in an attempt to avoid Japanese air searches. This hope was quickly scuttled when at 0949hrs lookouts on *Houston* spotted the first Japanese search aircraft. On this brilliant day with unlimited visibility, the Japanese strike force of 36 G4M and 24 G3M aircraft, all from their new base at Kendari, had no difficulty spotting their target. The Japanese aviators went for the cruisers. The bombers were all armed with 550- and 132-pound bombs; none carried torpedoes. Nine bombers devoted their attention to *Marblehead*. On their third run, they dropped their bombs. The cruiser was straddled but not hit. Nine more came after *Houston*, but these also achieved no hits. The third group of seven aircraft dropped their bombs on *Marblehead* at 1027hrs. Though they were only 132-pound bombs, the two that hit the lightly armored cruiser caused severe damage. The first hit forward and started a

Light cruiser *Marblehead* at Tjilatjap, Java, after she had been damaged by a Japanese high-level bombing attack in the Java Sea on February 4, 1942. This view shows the effect of an enemy bomb which struck her stern. The ship only possessed 1.5in. of horizontal armor, which allowed the small 132-pound bombs used by the Japanese to penetrate below decks and do critical damage. (US Naval History and Heritage Command)

During the campaign, US Navy submarines were not effective in defending against Japanese amphibious attacks. *Perch*, shown here, was one of the submarines ordered by Helfrich to concentrate off eastern Java to stop the Japanese invasion. Since the exact landing area of the Japanese was not known, the submarines were not deployed correctly, and they were unable to move quickly to the actual landing area. The Japanese and German navies would later learn the same lesson when they attempted to deploy submarines to repel amphibious invasions. *Perch* was detected on the night of March 1 some 35 miles north of Soerabaja. After intense attacks by as many as four IJN destroyers, the submarine was scuttled on March 3, but the entire crew was picked up by the Japanese. (US Naval History and Heritage Command)

fire; the second hit aft on the quarterdeck. It buckled the deck, and wrecked the steering room, jamming the rudder in a hard turn to port. A near miss near the port bow caused flooding. The cruiser was in bad shape. Fifteen crewmen were dead and 34 wounded; the ship was only able to steer in a tight circle, had a starboard list, and was on fire. Damage control efforts saved the ship, but she was no longer fit for combat duty.

The next attacks at 1117hrs again focused on *Houston*, but her captain skillfully evaded all bombs. At 1126hrs, it was the turn of *De Ruyter*, but she also evaded all bombs directed at her. The final attack at 1140hrs went after *Houston*. All but the final bomb missed, but the last bomb dropped scored a devastating hit. After glancing off the mainmast, it exploded over the main deck aft between the mainmast and the No. 3 8in. gun turret. It

blew a 12-foot hole in the deck and sent fragments into the lightly armored gun turret. These caused the powder bags inside to catch fire, killing the crew inside. Damage control efforts prevented the fire from spreading, but with 48 dead and 20 wounded, and her after 8in. turret out of action, *Houston* was badly damaged.

At 1225hrs, Doorman cancelled the operation and the Combined Striking Force headed west to Soerabaja. The two American cruisers were sent to Tjilatjap, where Hart had assembled all of the Asiatic Fleet's support ships. Hart believed that Doorman should have pressed the attack with his undamaged ships, and Doorman was rattled by the entire affair. The first operation of the Combined Striking Force ended in fiasco, primarily because of the direct route selected for the Allied force to use in the face of Japanese airpower. *Marblehead* was forced to go to Ceylon for repairs and would not return. *Houston*, even with one of her main battery turrets permanently out of action, remained in the fight.

The action on February 4 temporarily crippled Doorman's striking force. This meant that when a Japanese invasion force departed Staring Bay on February 6 with orders to occupy Makassar on southern Celebes, it was unopposed by Allied surface forces. The only defending unit in position was the American submarine *S-37*. She scored a rare early-war success for US Navy submarines by putting a torpedo into one of the IJN's most modern destroyers, the Kagero-class *Natsushio* on 8 February off Makassar. The following day, salvage efforts were abandoned, and the destroyer sank. On February 9, the Japanese landed at Makassar and quickly occupied this key port. The road to Java was open.

THE INVASION OF SUMATRA

By mid-February, Japanese plans in Southeast Asia were running ahead of schedule. The largest success to date was registered on February 15, when the British garrison on Singapore surrendered. This opened the way for the Japanese to invade Sumatra, the NEI's most important island from a resource perspective. The key objective was Palembang on southern

Carrier *Ryujo*, launched in 1931, had a checkered early career. By the start of the war, she had been modified to address stability issues, but was still considered a second-line carrier because of her small flight deck and small elevators which made efficient aircraft-handling operations impossible. She was assigned to support the Philippines and NEI invasions and embarked 16 A5M4 "Claude" fighters and 18 B5N1/2 "Kate" attack planes. Despite her limitations, and only being able to launch small groups of aircraft at once, *Ryujo* was effective during the campaign. Her Kates accounted for several Allied merchant ships, but when given the chance to attack the ABDA striking force on February 15, her aircraft hit nothing in four separate strikes. On February 17, her Kates atoned for their earlier poor performance and sank the Dutch destroyer *Van Nes* with three bombs. On March 1, her aircraft assisted in the sinking of US Navy destroyer *Pope*. *Ryujo* went on to create more havoc against Allied shipping in the Indian Ocean in April before being sunk by US Navy carrier aircraft near Guadalcanal in August. (Yamato Museum)

Sumatra. Not only were there two major airfields nearby, but most importantly for the Japanese, it was the site of two major oil refineries and large oil fields. Though located well inland, Palembang was vulnerable to a seaborne invasion, since it was located on the Moesi River which was navigable to large ships.

Released from covering convoys to Malaya to support the campaign against Singapore, the IJN's Western Force prepared a large operation to strike at Palembang. To escort the invasion force of 25 transports, Vice Admiral Ozawa collected five heavy cruisers, light cruiser *Sendai*, and 11 destroyers. Light carrier *Ryujo* (with 12 fighters and 15 B5N1 "Kate" attack aircraft embarked), was also shifted from the Eastern Force to provide support. This invasion force departed Cam Ranh Bay in Indochina on February 10 and headed south.

The Allies had been watching this major concentration and made plans to stop it. A submarine attack by a US Navy submarine on February 11 was unsuccessful, as were two British air attacks. Doorman's Striking Force was also ordered to move to the small Dutch naval base of Oosthaven on the southeastern tip of Sumatra to prepare to intercept. Vice Admiral Helfrich, who formally took over command of ABDA naval forces on February 12, allocated him what on the surface appeared to be a formidable force – Dutch cruisers *De Ruyter*, *Java*, and *Tromp*, British heavy cruiser *Exeter*, Australian

cruiser *Hobart*, six US Navy destroyers, and four Dutch destroyers. With this significantly reinforced force, Helfrich ordered Doorman to attack the Japanese invasion convoy. Accordingly, the Striking Force departed Oosthaven on the afternoon of February 14.

Bad luck dogged the operation from the start. In the early morning hours of the 15th, the Dutch destroyer *Van Ghent* ran hard aground in the Stolze Strait between Bank and Billiton Islands. The ship was a total loss, and Doorman assigned another Dutch destroyer to take off the crew and scuttle the ship. The element of surprise was lost hours later, when at 0923hrs a Japanese cruiser floatplane sighted the Striking Force. Air attacks soon followed. The first was at 1020hrs when four B5N1 "Kates" from *Ryujo* selected *Exeter* for attention. The aircraft dropped 550-pound bombs from high altitude, but scored no hits. This first attack was followed by a much larger effort by 23 G3Ms flying from Borneo. Dropping from high level, they only caused minor damage to two American destroyers. Seven more B5N1s made an appearance at 1130hrs and attacked *Exeter*, again causing only minor damage. At this point, Doorman cancelled the operation. However, the ordeal of the Striking Force was not over. Two more groups of land-based bombers with 44 aircraft in total arrived to make high-level attacks. Again, no hits were scored. Also unsuccessful were 19 B5N1s from *Ryujo* in three groups. The day-long encounter between the Striking Force and the IJN's Air Force ended in a draw. No ships were hit except by near misses, and no aircraft were shot down. But the largest Allied naval force gathered to date was forced to abort its attempt to thwart a Japanese invasion. As a result, the invasion of Palembang proceeded unimpeded. Its success forced the Allied evacuation of Sumatra.

Japanese air power continued to dominate the theater. On February 15, Japanese bombers from Kendari attacked an Allied reinforcement convoy bound for Timor. Though no hits were scored, mainly because the bombers

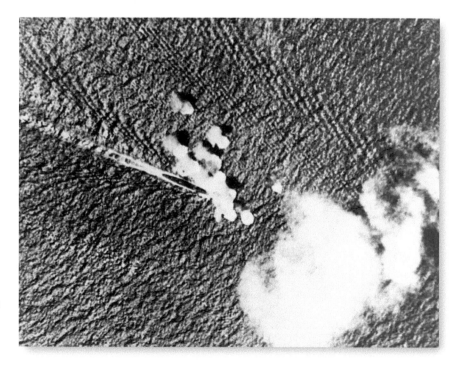

Dutch destroyer *Van Nes* was a victim of Japanese naval air power. On February 17, the destroyer was escorting a Dutch transport sent to evacuate the garrison from Billiton Island. After embarking the troops, the two ships were spotted by a Japanese cruiser floatplane and then subjected to concentrated air attack by 15 G3M Nells and ten Kates from *Ryujo*. The destroyer was hit by three bombs from *Ryujo's* aircraft and quickly sank with the loss of 68 crewmen. (US Naval History and Heritage Command)

Battle of the Badoeng Strait, February 19–20, 1942

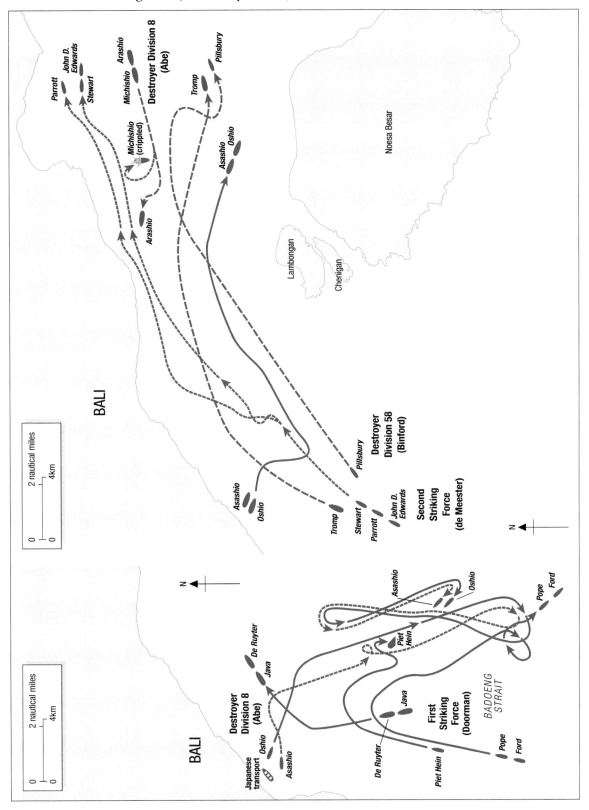

In a remarkable display of marksmanship, Japanese dive-bombers hit the maneuvering destroyer *Peary* five times in Darwin harbor on the morning of February 19. The ship was surrounded by blazing oil, as shown in this view. Only 53 of her crew survived; another 80 died. (US Naval History and Heritage Command)

went after *Houston* instead of the slower and less maneuverable transports, this was the first air attack on Allied ships south of the Malay barrier. The convoy was ordered to return to Darwin, Australia, which was the main base used to funnel reinforcements and aircraft into the NEI. On February 17, land-based bombers and B5N1s from *Ryujo* sank a Dutch transport and destroyer evacuating troops from Billiton Island with heavy loss of life.

The threat from Japanese air power increased significantly with the arrival of the Kido Butai into the area in mid-February. The force consisted of four of the six carriers which had attacked Pearl Harbor – *Akagi*, *Kaga*, *Hiryu*, and *Soryu*. With the help of land-based bombers from Kendari, the Japanese decided to use their carrier force to neutralize Darwin. The harbor was full of potential targets on 19 February – 47 warships and merchants of various types. The air defenses of this important base were minimal and proved ineffective against the 188 aircraft sent from the four Japanese carriers. The Japanese aircraft hit the ships in the harbor, sinking nine (including the American destroyer *Peary*), and ravaged the shore facilities. Fifty-four land-based bombers completed the devastation, attacking the two nearby airfields. The only major link to the NEI had been temporality neutralized.

THE BATTLE OF THE BADOENG STRAIT

The Japanese crept closer to Java. On February 20, they landed a regiment on Timor Island. The defending garrison was defeated in three days. The loss of the island and its airfield meant the transfer route for aircraft flying from Australia to the NEI was cut.

A more immediate threat to Java was a Japanese operation targeted at Bali, located just to the east of Java. If the Japanese could seize the airfield at Denpesar, they could ratchet up the pressure on facilities on Java and dominate the southern approaches to the island, cutting off all reinforcement.

The Japanese plan to deliver the landing force to Sanoer Roads on the southeastern coast of Bali on the Badoeng Strait was risky, since it was so close to major Allied air and naval bases. The landing force was put aboard two transports, and these were escorted by four Asashio-class destroyers. Per Japanese doctrine, the landing would take place at night, allowing the transports to leave early in the day. Light cruiser *Nagara* and three more destroyers were positioned to the north to provide distant support. This force departed Makassar on February 17.

If ABDA ever had a real chance of repelling a Japanese invasion, or at least gaining a local victory, the Japanese invasion of Bali was that opportunity. However, the timing of the operation caught Helfrich off guard, since, as usual, the bulk of his naval units were assigned to escorting convoys. He had to quickly re-assemble a striking force and send it into the Badoeng Strait. Because of the difficulty in doing so quickly, and not wanting to take the extra time to bring all available forces into a single striking force to overwhelm the Japanese, the plan Helfrich came up with remains hard to understand or defend. The available Allied ships were at Soerabaja, Tjilatjap, and Rantai Bay on the southeastern coast of Sumatra. The massing of the invasion force at Makassar was known to Helfrich, but its destination remained unclear. In spite of this awareness, Helfrich was caught off guard when the actual Japanese objective was revealed to be Bali. He and Doorman conferred on February 17 how to handle this, and devised a plan for a counterattack on the night of February 19–20. Because the ships were coming from different bases, the plan was for the attack to develop in three waves. The first wave was comprised of the available ships from Tjilatjap which would enter the Badoeng Strait from the south, conduct its attack, and then continue north and head to Soerabaja. This force included the light cruisers *De Rutyer* and *Java*, Dutch destroyers *Kortenaer* and *Piet Hein*, and American destroyers *Pope* and *John D. Ford*. The second wave was comprised of the ships from Soerabaja and Rantai Bay. The light cruiser *Tromp* would lead the four American destroyers from Rantai Bay (*Stewart*, *Parrott*, *John D. Edwards*, and *Pillsbury*) up from the south into the Badoeng Strait to attack the Japanese before returning to Soerabaja by way of the Lombok Strait. The third wave was comprised of nine Dutch torpedo boats, which would also attack from the south.

The plan was flawed on a number of counts. Allied aircraft had reported a much larger force – two cruisers, up to six destroyers, and four transports, making it essential for Helfrich to mass his forces. The landing had already occurred in the early morning hours of February 19 and no Allied naval units could arrive in time to change that fact. Helfrich should have united his available ships into what might have been an overwhelming force. But he did not think time was adequate to affect a rendezvous of the ships from several bases, and any such rendezvous would have to have been conducted at night, increasing the degree of difficulty. In any event, the inclusion of the torpedo boats into a united striking force was impossible, due to considerations of speed and endurance. Helfrich seems to have viewed his attack as a series of raids, rather than an all-out battle. If true, this is also hard to explain, since raids were not going to stop the Japanese.

The Japanese landings went off at 0200hrs on February 19 without problems. The battle ashore was resolved quickly in favor of the Japanese, who captured the airfield intact. However, at daylight, a series of air attacks began which unhinged the Japanese plan. By 0800hrs, 12 heavy bombers had attacked the two transports. No hits were scored, but the attacks delayed unloading. This was followed by an attack by two A-24 dive-bombers (the USAAF version of the Navy's SBD Dauntless) which scored a hit on the transport *Sagami Maru*. In the afternoon, the Japanese admiral in charge of the operation ordered the ship back to Makassar, escorted by the destroyers *Arashio* and *Michishio*.

This left transport *Sasago Maru* still unloading, escorted by the destroyers *Asashio* and *Oshio*. Finally, after dark, the group departed the

Piet Hein, shown here in drydock in Soerabaja, was one of the seven RNN destroyers available at the beginning of the war. Following the fall of the Netherlands in May 1940, it was increasingly difficult to keep the ships of the East Indies Squadron operational. (US Naval History and Heritage Command)

anchorage, but an hour later the transport returned to unload its eight landing craft for the use of the army detachment ashore. *Asashio* was steaming near the transport and *Oshio* was located some 3,000 yards to the northwest.

The first Allied attack wave arrived in the area of the anchorage just before 2230hrs. This group was under the command of Doorman. He deployed his two cruisers some 5,500 yards ahead of his destroyers. Their orders were to engage with gunfire, while the destroyers would attack the disrupted Japanese with torpedoes. This was a poor plan, as a surprise torpedo attack, followed up by a gunnery attack, would probably have been more effective, just like at Balikpapan. The cruisers rushed toward the Japanese at 27 knots. *Java* sighted *Asashio* first, but the Dutch were slow to open fire. At 2230hrs, *Asashio* spotted *Java* and she attempted to illuminate the cruiser with her searchlight. The resulting engagement was very short and indecisive; giving credence to the notion that Helfrich intended this as a raid only. *Java* engaged the destroyer at 2,200 yards, and a round hit and destroyed her searchlight, killing four and wounding 11. Another round hit *Sasago Maru*. In return, *Java* took a 5in. shell aft. With this, the Dutch cruisers raced off to the north and broke contact. Neither *De Ruyter* nor *Oshio* had fired a shot.

Minutes later, the Allied destroyers arrived with *Piet Hein* some 5,000 yards ahead of the two American ships. *Oshio* was the first to gain contact, sighting the Dutch destroyer at 2235hrs some 6,000 yards to the south. The Japanese turned to the southeast to engage. *Piet Hein* took *Sasago Maru* under fire with three torpedoes and her 4.7in. main battery. Once clear of the smoke laid by the Dutch destroyer, *John D. Ford* also fired three torpedoes and directed 4in. shells at the transport. The last destroyer in line, *Pope*, fired two more torpedoes at the transport. Both American ships claimed hits, but neither scored. At 2240hrs, *Asashio* engaged *Piet Hein* at a range of only 1,600 yards and subsequently also brought the American destroyers under fire. *Pope* fired two torpedoes at what was probably *Asashio*, but missed. To avoid a collision with the Dutch ship and evade *Asashio* to the east, the two American destroyers swung to the west. This left *Piet Hein* on her own; after launching two more torpedoes at *Asashio*, she took a 5in. shell in her aft boiler room. More hits followed, which set the Dutch destroyer afire and brought it to a stop. Before damage control measures could fully restore power, the ship was hit by a torpedo from *Asashio* at 2246hrs. The effect was devastating; the Dutch ship quickly capsized to starboard and sank with the loss of 64 crewmen including her skipper.

After finishing off *Piet Hein*, *Asashio* headed north to engage the American destroyers. The skippers of the American ships had decided to abandon their orders to proceed north through the strait, and headed to the east instead. Both *Asashio* and *Oshio* regained contact just before 2300hrs and brought the American ships under heavy fire with the aid of searchlights. The Americans delayed firing back to make sure the two contacts were not the Dutch cruisers, and then engaged the Japanese with guns and torpedoes. Neither side hit the other. The Japanese lost the American destroyers in a smoke screen, and by 2310hrs the American had escaped to the southeast.

By the time the second wave arrived, *Oshio* and *Asashio* were circling off shore to the east of the damaged *Sasago Maru*. *Arashio* and *Michishio* were coming south, and the covering force led by cruiser *Nagara* was also steaming to the area. The Allied second wave was led by the four American destroyers with the Dutch cruiser *Tromp* following five miles in the rear. The cruiser's captain was in tactical command, and he planned to have *Tromp* finish off the cripples resulting from the destroyers' torpedo attack.

The American destroyers steamed into the anchorage area at 25 knots. They expected to be facing a much larger Japanese force; efforts to contact the two American destroyers in the previous wave provided no information. At 0135hrs, *Stewart* sighted a possible contact to port. Within minutes, she and *Parrot* fired six torpedoes into the anchorage with *Pillsbury* adding another three. All 15 torpedoes missed, and it's unlikely they were even fired at a real target. *Asashio* and *Oshio* finally spotted the Americans and steered to engage. At 0143hrs, *Stewart* sighted the Japanese and used her searchlight and 4in. guns to engage. The Japanese returned an intense fire, and at 0145hrs fired torpedoes from 3,500 yards at the Americans. The first damage inflicted by either side was at 0146hrs, when a couple of Japanese 5in. shells hit *Stewart*. The damaged *Stewart* turned to the northeast, which disrupted the American column.

The Japanese destroyers shifted their attention to *Tromp* when she used her searchlight to signal the American destroyers. From a range of some 3,300 yards, *Asashio* pounded *Tromp* with 11 5in. shells causing extensive damage to her topside equipment. *Oshio* missed the cruiser with a salvo of torpedoes. At 0216hrs, *Tromp* landed a 5.9in. shell on *Oshio*'s bridge, killing seven. *Tromp* and all four American destroyers continued steaming to the northeast.

The next phase of the battle featured *Arashio* and *Michishio*, which were headed south to the sound of the guns. At 0215hrs, *Michishio* spotted two contacts, and used her searchlight to illuminate them. They were *Stewart* and *John D. Edwards*. Both American destroyers, joined by *Pillsbury*, took *Michishio* under fire with their 4in. guns and six torpedoes from *John D. Edwards*. *Pillsbury* unleashed three more torpedoes. The surprised Japanese were caught in a deadly crossfire. All the torpedoes missed, but a 4in. shell hit the destroyer's Number 2 5in. mount, destroying it and killing the crew. Another shell hit the bridge, wounding *Michishio*'s captain. *Tromp* followed this up with three more shells in the Japanese destroyer's engine room, which brought her to a halt. The Allied ships did not linger to finish off the crippled destroyer, but continued to the northeast and broke contact.

The Allied third wave attack was totally ineffective. Of the nine torpedo boats ordered to attack, only eight made it to the battle area. They entered the strait in two groups of four. One group gained no contact and the second sighted possible targets proceeding at high speed but could not get

Destroyer *Stewart* was sent to Soerabaja after the battle of the Badoeng Strait for repairs. As the drydock she was in was being pumped out on February 20, the ship capsized because of poor bracing. The drydock was scuttled on March 2 before the Japanese occupied the city. In February 1943, the ship was raised by the IJN and put into service as *Patrol Boat 102*. She is shown here after the war, having been returned to US Navy custody and given here original hull number. (US Naval History and Heritage Command)

into an attack position. All the torpedo boats returned to Soerabaja having achieved nothing.

Both sides thought they had inflicted severe damage on the other. In reality, the Allies had lost a fine opportunity to inflict a local defeat on the Japanese. In the first wave attack, Doorman's inept tactical plan squandered the Allies' best hope of victory. The two Japanese destroyers were handled aggressively and well. First, they fought off an attack by two Dutch light cruisers which failed to press home their advantage, then they overwhelmed a single Dutch destroyer, and finally they chased off two American destroyers. The second wave gained temporary surprise but failed to press its advantage. The cost of the battle was considerable for the Allies. One destroyer (*Piet Hein*) was sunk and the light cruiser *Tromp* was forced to Australia for repairs, which took her out of the campaign. The American destroyer *Stewart* was sent to a drydock in Soerabaja for repairs. Unfortunately, the drydock collapsed and *Stewart*'s fighting days were over. She was later salvaged by the Japanese and served in the IJN as a patrol boat for the remainder of the war. The Japanese believed they had done more damage, claiming two of the three destroyers sunk in the first wave with the third heavily damaged. Total Japanese claims were two cruisers and three destroyers sunk and two destroyers heavily damaged. Yamamoto accepted these claims as ground truth, which seemingly accounted for a large proportion of ABDA's remaining assets. The battle was not without loss for the Japanese. *Michishio* was heavily damaged and was towed to Makassar for repairs which took the better part of 1942. *Asashio* was lightly damaged, and *Oshio* suffered moderate damage. Overall, the battle was another example of Allied naval ineffectiveness. They were caught off balance and reacted too slowly to stop another Japanese landing, and when they did show up, they were outfought by a smaller Japanese force.

THE JAPANESE APPROACH TO JAVA

The Japanese landings on Sumatra in the west and Bali in the east left Java as the only major island in the NEI still held by the Allies. The Japanese had maintained a quick pace in their advance through the NEI, and with their final prize now within reach, they commenced a plan to seize Java before it could be reinforced. This called for landings on both the eastern and western parts of the island.

The first to move was the Western Force. It departed Cam Ranh Bay on February 18 with an invasion fleet of 56 transports. On board was the headquarters of the 16th Army, responsible for the occupation of Java, an entire infantry division, and another infantry regiment. A large close escort force was provided which consisted of three light cruisers and 13 destroyers. The covering force consisted of Ozawa's flagship heavy cruiser *Chokai*, the four Mogami-class heavy cruisers of Sentai 7 under Rear Admiral Kurita, and several destroyers. The light carrier *Ryujo* remained with the Western Force.

On February 19, the Eastern Force departed Jolo in the northern Celebes Sea with an invasion fleet of 41 transports carrying another complete infantry division. The IJN provided an escort built around Rear Admiral

Seaplane carrier *Mizuho* was flagship of the 11th Seaplane Tender Division, which played an important role in the NEI campaign. Beginning with the occupation of Menado in January, she was active for the entire campaign culminating in the landing on eastern Java in late February. Against spotty Allied air resistance, these ships provided effective air cover, though they carried only floatplanes. On March 1, together with seaplane carrier *Chitose*, F1M "Pete" floatplanes gained a near miss on destroyer *Pope* with 132-pound bombs which slowed her down and led to her destruction. Following the NEI campaign, *Mizuho* was sunk on May 1, 1942 in Japanese home waters by the American submarine *Drum*. Had she not been sunk, she would have most likely been converted into an aircraft carrier. (Yamato Museum)

Takagi's two heavy cruisers from Sentai 5 and the Destroyer Squadron 2 under Rear Admiral Tanaka. Close escort for the invasion convoy consisted of Destroyer Squadron 4 under Rear Admiral Nishimura reinforced with four minesweepers, six submarine chasers, and a minelayer.

Both invasion convoys were under command of Vice Admiral Takahashi. He held a reserve of heavy cruisers *Ashigara* and *Myoko* and two destroyers north of Java. South of Java was Kondo's support force with battleships *Kongo* and *Haruna*, three heavy cruisers, and several destroyers. Also assigned the mission of picking off Allied units attempting to flee from or reinforce Java was the Kido Butai with four fleet carriers, two battleships, two heavy cruisers, and a destroyer squadron led by a light cruiser.

The massing of the two invasion convoys was known to the Allies, and Helfrich prepared his forces to repel both Japanese invasion forces. On February 21, he created two separate striking forces to accomplish this mission. His stated reason for doing so was because adequate fuel no longer existed at either of the two major bases to supply the entire Allied force. The Western Striking Force was commanded by Royal Australian Navy Commodore Collins and consisted of one heavy cruiser (*Exeter*), three light cruisers (Australian *Hobart*, British *Dragon* and *Danae*), five British, and one Dutch destroyers. The force was based at Tandjong Priok near Batavia. On February 24, it was reinforced by the Australian light cruiser *Perth*. The Eastern Striking Force was under Doorman's command and consisted of one heavy cruiser (*Houston*), two light cruisers (*De Ruyter* and *Java*), three Dutch, and four American destroyers.

An American flying boat gained contact on the Eastern Force on February 25. It was the closer of the two invasion convoys to Java and since it was headed for the economic and political center of Java, it demanded an all-out response. Helfrich ordered the cruisers *Exeter* and *Perth*, and destroyers *Electra, Encounter*, and *Jupiter* to detach from the Western Striking Force to reinforce Doorman's Eastern Striking Force. Determined to stop the invasion, and knowing that if the Japanese invasion force got ashore that the Royal Netherlands East Indies Army would be quickly defeated, Helfrich decided that he would order Doorman to defeat the Japanese Eastern Force, and then to steam to the other end of Java to defeat the Western Force. It was a flight of fancy, but Doorman was left to execute this vision as best he could.

Doorman was determined to aggressively engage the Japanese, but possessed no adequate intelligence on their location. On the night of February 26, he took his force out to make a sweep around Madoera Island. Finding nothing, he returned in the morning to Soerabaja only to be subjected to the daily air attack. The Allied defense of Java reached its climactic moment. Helfrich received a report at 1155hrs of the location of the Japanese invasion convoy. It was headed southwest to its landing area west of Soerabaja. This report was sent to Doorman at 1250hrs with the order to sortie, execute a night attack, and then to head to Tandjong Priok. This was followed at 2055hrs with order from Helfrich reading "You must continue attacks until the enemy is destroyed."

Doorman assembled the skippers of all the ships in his force that afternoon to go over the plan for the coming battle. The Striking Force would sweep around Madoera Island to the north, then steam to the west. The British and Dutch destroyers were deployed in the vanguard, then the cruisers, followed by the American destroyers. When contact was made with the Japanese, the vanguard destroyers would attack, followed by the cruisers engaging targets from a distance, and then the American destroyers would execute a torpedo attack.

Doorman's plan left much to the imagination of the American, Australian, and British participants. No provision was made to use his cruiser floatplanes, which were left ashore so as not to become a fire hazard in a night battle. The one-hour conference did not cover the essentials of communications plans or detailed tactical plans. In the words of an American destroyer skipper, "The Allied Force was little more than a column of strange task groups which entered the battle with a vague general directive and no specific missions." Doorman was going to go to sea for a do-or-die battle with the Japanese without a coherent battle plan, with little ability to communicate with his force, and with little idea as to the enemy's dispositions and intentions. It was not a recipe for success.

The Combined Striking Force departed Soerabaja at 1800hrs and conducted a sweep around Madoera Island. After reaching the Sapoedi Strait at about 0130hrs on February 27, Doorman turned back to the east to return to Soerabaja as planned. Without any intelligence on the Japanese, and having completed his planned sweep, Doorman decided at 1240hrs to return to Soerabaja to refuel. At 1425hrs, just as *De Ruyter* was steaming through the Dutch minefields protecting Soerabaja, Doorman received a series of electrifying reports from a Dutch flying boat – the Japanese invasion convoy was only some 50 miles northwest of Soerabaja! Doorman immediately reversed course to the north and ordered the rest of his force to follow. With

Nachi, shown here in March 1942 just after the completion of the NEI campaign, was Rear Admiral Takagi's flagship after Myoko was damaged on January 4, 1942 by USAAF B-17s near Davao, Mindanao. For the remainder of the campaign, Nachi and Haguro were the centerpieces of the covering force for a series of invasions in the eastern NEI. Given a chance to engage Allied ships on February 27 at the battle of the Java Sea, she sank the Dutch cruiser Java with a torpedo. On March 1, she participated in the destruction of British heavy cruiser Exeter. Nachi survived until November 1944, when she was sunk by US Navy carrier aircraft in Manila Bay. (Yamato Museum)

any luck, the Allied force could catch the Japanese invasion force before it delivered its troops ashore.

The approach to contact was not smooth for either side. The Japanese invasion convoy was making for Kragan, located to the west of Soerabaja. At 1000hrs, the convoy was passing Bawean Island. Since he was not expecting major opposition, Takagi had failed to concentrate his forces. Finally realizing that he needed to reinforce the convoy's escorts, Takagi ordered most of Tanaka's ships to join with the convoy at 0930hrs. Upon hearing from Nishimura that the convoy was under air attack, Takagi ordered his two heavy cruisers and last four destroyers south to reinforce the convoy. At 1100hrs, Takagi received information that Doorman's force of five cruisers and six destroyers was in the path of the invasion convoy. Takagi launched one of Nachi's floatplanes to get additional information and increased his speed to the south. This aircraft reported that the enemy force was headed east at 1235hrs, and a short time later relayed that the force had changed course to the south. In the meantime, Nishimura ordered the convoy to head west until the danger was neutralized.

The Japanese were temporarily confused, but were not going to let Doorman get a clean shot at the convoy. As soon as Doorman had headed south, Takagi ordered the landing to continue and brought the convoy back to the southwest at 1340hrs. When Doorman reversed his course and headed north, the floatplane from Nachi quickly relayed this to Takagi. The convoy was again ordered to head to the northwest and Takagi took measures to concentrate his force by ordering his cruisers to increase speed to the south to link up with Tanaka's and Nishimura's destroyer squadrons. Nishimura left two destroyers with the convoy, but took his flagship and six more destroyers to engage the Allies. Though not fully concentrated, the Japanese force totaled two heavy cruisers, two light cruisers, and 14 destroyers. They held superiority in 8in. guns, were deficient in 6in. guns, but held a considerable advantage in torpedo tubes.

Battle of the Java Sea: First Phase, 1555–1720hrs

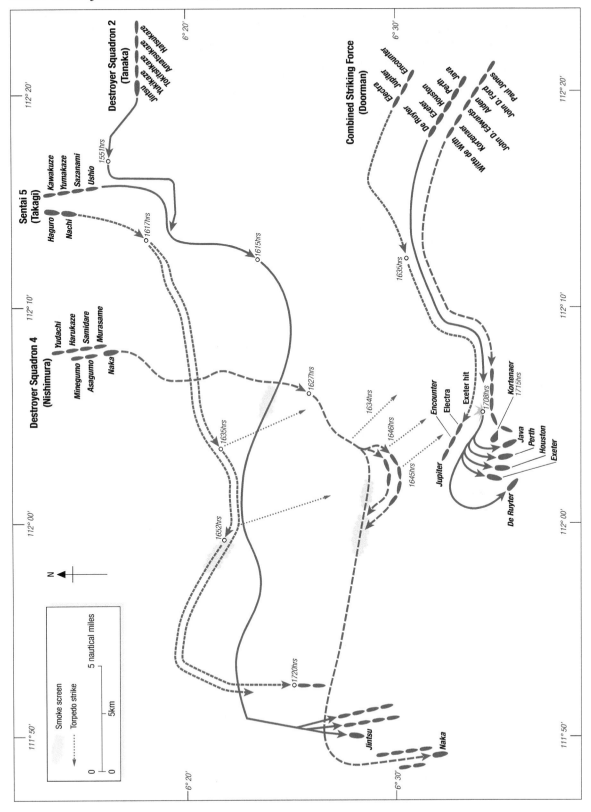

HAGURO IN ACTION (PP. 58–59)

Heavy cruisers _Nachi_ and _Haguro_ were the backbone of the Japanese force at Java Sea. With their powerful 8in. guns and torpedo batteries, they were the most powerful ships present on either side. The initial phase of the battle featured a long-range gunnery duel between _Nachi_ and _Haguro_ and the Allied cruisers. In this view, the 8in. turrets of _Haguro_ are elevated **(1)** and firing at long range while splashes from Allied cruisers explode near the Japanese ship **(2)**. To supplement the long-range gunnery of his cruisers, Vice Admiral Takagi decided to bring the long-range Type 93 torpedo into play. As part of a massive torpedo barrage, _Haguro_ prepared to fire her eight starboard side torpedoes. The cruiser has trained her two starboard quadruple launchers and has fired her torpedoes at 1652hrs as evident in this scene **(3)**. Not evident in this scene is that fact that several of the torpedoes exploded only a few hundred yards from the ship creating enormous columns of water. The problem was with the fuzing of the torpedoes which was a problem throughout the battle. Cruiser _Nachi_, leading the column, was unable to contribute another eight torpedoes because her torpedo crew had left a valve open which bled the air pressure required to launch them. Of the 39 Type 93 torpedoes fired in this barrage, only one hit. This blow was deadly though; at 1713hrs, one of _Haguro_'s torpedoes hit the Dutch destroyer _Kortenaer_ amidships sinking the ship in minutes.

THE BATTLE OF THE JAVA SEA

Doorman elected to place his force into three parallel columns as he headed to the northwest to engage the Japanese. The center column consisted of his five cruisers, led by his flagship *De Ruyter*. Flanking the main column were two columns of destroyers, one comprised of the three British destroyers and the other with the six Dutch and American destroyers. The Dutch *Kortenaer* had boiler problems which reduced her top speed to 26 knots, and she fell behind. Also left tagging behind were the four American destroyers which had been given an order from Doorman not to pass the Dutch destroyers. The inability of the Combined Striking Force to exceed 26 knots became a key factor in the battle. Doorman's slower speed meant he was unlikely to outmaneuver the Japanese and made any uncontested thrust against the transport group even more unlikely.

The day phase

The two sides continued to close. At 1610hrs, *Electra* spotted the westernmost Japanese group, the light cruiser *Jintsu* and her four destroyers. Minutes later, *Electra* also reported the two Japanese heavy cruisers. At the same time, the Japanese groups spotted Doorman's force. At 1615hrs, *Jintsu* began the battle, firing her 5.5in. main battery at *Electra*. The range was 18,000 yards, close to the maximum range for this weapon. Despite this, the Japanese gunners were able to straddle their target. This opening salvo was followed by *Nachi* and *Haguro* opening fire with their 8in. guns on the Allied heavy cruisers at 28,000 yards. Their initial rounds were well short. Per Japanese doctrine, Takagi was content to fight a long-range gunnery duel, since he believed his gunnery was more effective at extended ranges and to limit the ability of the Allies to respond with the 6in. guns aboard three of their cruisers. Without waiting for orders, *Exeter*'s captain ordered his ship to fire back at 1617hrs, and he was quickly joined by *Houston*'s forward two 8in. turrets. Both Japanese and Allied long-range fire was ineffective. *Houston* claimed hits; at 1631hrs a Japanese 8in. shell hit *De Ruyter*, but it was a dud. The fire of the Japanese cruisers was accurate enough to place the occasional straddle, but at 26,000 yards or more, the likelihood of a hit was small.

The two cruiser forces continued on generally parallel courses. Takagi was unwilling to close the range and continued his tactic of executing long-range gunnery attacks. Doorman needed to close the range to bring his 6in. cruisers into play. With 25 6in. guns on his three cruisers, this was his only area of advantage. But once again, his slower speed forced Doorman to react to Japanese maneuvering. To avoid the prospect of the Japanese cruisers "crossing his T" (a tactic in which one side crosses perpendicular to the other, allowing the passing force to bring its entire broadside to bear, while the group being crossed could only bring its forward guns to bear), Doorman ordered a course change at 1635hrs due west. This temporarily eased the possibility that the Japanese heavy cruisers would "cross his T", but it also failed to close the range sufficiently for the 6in. cruisers to join the gunnery duel.

As the heavy cruisers exchanged fire, Takagi planned to bring the IJN's secret weapon into play – the long-range Type 93 torpedo. The massed torpedo attack would be conducted at ranges beyond which the Allies

EXETER IN DISTRESS (PP. 62–63)

After an hour of inconclusive long-range gunnery, little damage had been done to either side. At about 1700hrs, the Japanese closed the range to seek a decision. At the same time, they concentrated fire on *Exeter* and *Houston*, the two largest Allied ships. At 1708hrs, *Exeter* **(1)** was hit by an 8in. shell from *Haguro*. Japanese gunnery was accurate, as shown by the salvo which bracketed the cruiser with the two shell explosions in this view **(2)** and the third shell which has hit the ship. The results of the single 8in. shell hit were catastrophic and went a long way to deciding the battle. The shell hit the shield of one of the 4in. twin mounts before penetrating through an armored hatch into a boiler room ventilator. The shell went through A Boiler Room flinging shrapnel in all directions and then penetrated

into B Boiler Room causing further damage. The result was to place both starboard boilers out of action and damage to a superheater placed the four aft boilers out of commission. Superheated steam filled the aft boiler room killing all but one of the engine room crew. The loss of six of the ship's eight boilers reduced speed to a mere six knots. The reduced power also brought her main battery out of action. In this view, *Exeter* is making an emergency turn to avoid a collision with the cruisers behind her. Heavy smoke is already coming out of both her stacks indicating the damage below in the boiler rooms **(3)**. *Exeter* is firing her last 8in. salvo before her turrets lost power **(4)**. *Houston* was some 600 yards behind *Exeter*, and she is making an emergency turn to port **(5)**.

expected an attack, and the Japanese expected the results to be devastating. Nishimura maneuvered his light cruiser and six destroyers to comply with Takagi's order to execute a torpedo attack. At 1634hrs, his ships were the first to launch when *Naka* fired four torpedoes at 15,000 yards range. Between 1640 and 1645hrs, his destroyers sent another 23 weapons toward the Combined Striking Force. In addition to Nishimura's ships, light cruiser *Jintsu* fired four at 1635hrs and *Haguro* fired a salvo of eight at 1652hrs from 22,000 yards. *Nachi* was unable to contribute another eight because her neglectful torpedo crew had left a valve open which bled the air pressure required to launch the torpedoes. The 39 torpedoes reaped a disappointing return for Takagi. At 1713hrs, one hit *Kortenaer* amidships. According to a nearby American destroyer skipper, the Dutch destroyer disappeared in under two minutes.

The destruction of *Kortenaer* and the increasing effectiveness of Japanese cruiser gunnery threw Doorman's force into chaos. In the first hour of the battle, the two Japanese heavy cruisers fired 1,271 8in. rounds. Eventually, this weight of fire would score. In addition to the initial hit on *De Ruyter*, which was a dud, another shell hit *Houston* at 1706hrs – it was also a dud. The next hit at 1708hrs was on *Exeter* and was probably the most important of the entire battle. The shell, probably from *Haguro*, penetrated to a boiler room and exploded. The final effect was to force six of the ship's eight boilers off line, which reduced speed to 11 knots and temporarily knocked out power to the main battery. To avoid a collision with the cruisers behind him, *Exeter*'s captain ordered the cruiser, now billowing smoke, to make an immediate turn to port. The following three cruisers followed suit, since they thought they had missed a signal from *De Ruyter* which was leading the column. The Allied column disintegrated; *De Ruyter* continued toward the Japanese and *Perth* laid a smokescreen to cover the wounded *Exeter*. Doorman was forced to turn his flagship around to reorganize his force. To give him the time he needed, he ordered the three British destroyers to execute a torpedo attack.

Haguro was the undisputed star performer of the battle of the Java Sea. She was responsible for hitting the British heavy cruiser *Exeter* with an 8in. shell which put her out of action, then torpedoing Dutch destroyer *Kortenaer*. In the final phase of the battle, she hit *De Ruyter* with a torpedo that led to her sinking which brought the battle to a close. *Haguro*'s long wartime career was brought to an end in the Malacca Strait on May 16, 1945 at the hands of British destroyers. (Yamato Museum)

First blood in the battle of the Java Sea was the torpedoing of destroyer *Kortenaer*. The Type 93 hit amidships broke the ship in two, and both halves were vertical within 90 seconds. The stern section sank at once, but the bow section did not sink for another five minutes, giving the crew time to get into the water. Of the 153 men in the crew, 115 survived the torpedoing. (Netherlands Institute for Military History)

It took until 1725hrs for Doorman to reestablish control. *De Ruyter* led the other cruisers, less *Exeter*, and the four American destroyers to the northeast. Twenty minutes later, the reduced Allied force was headed north and emerged from the smoke to find itself in more trouble. Takagi was kept informed of the plight of Doorman's force by his floatplanes, which remained up for almost the entire battle. Takagi decided to press the attack on the Allied force, which looked to be in utter disarray. To finish the Allies off, he ordered another massed torpedo attack. This barrage totaled an amazing 98 torpedoes, with their primary target being *Exeter*. The attack was launched from various ranges – *Nachi* and *Haguro* contributed eight each from 27,000 yards at 1754hrs; *Naka* launched four at 1750hrs from 18,500 yards; and *Jintsu* launched four from 20,000 yards at 1754hrs. The eight destroyers of Destroyer Squadron 2 closed to 15,000 yards before each launched a full salvo. Four of the destroyers from Nishimura's Destroyer Squadron 4 launched their full loads at 1804hrs after closing to 10,000 yards. Nishimura's last two destroyers, *Asagumo* and *Minegumo*, closed to 6,500 yards before one launched, with the other being unable to get a firing solution. Amazingly, none of these 98 weapons hit their target. The second massed Japanese torpedo attack was a complete failure.

As the Japanese destroyers closed for their attack, the three British destroyers emerged from the smoke. *Electra* was in front and was soon engaged with Tanaka's Destroyer Squadron 2. *Electra*'s veteran crew fought well against heavy odds. The British destroyers hit Tanaka's

Battle of the Java Sea: Second Phase, 1720–1810hrs

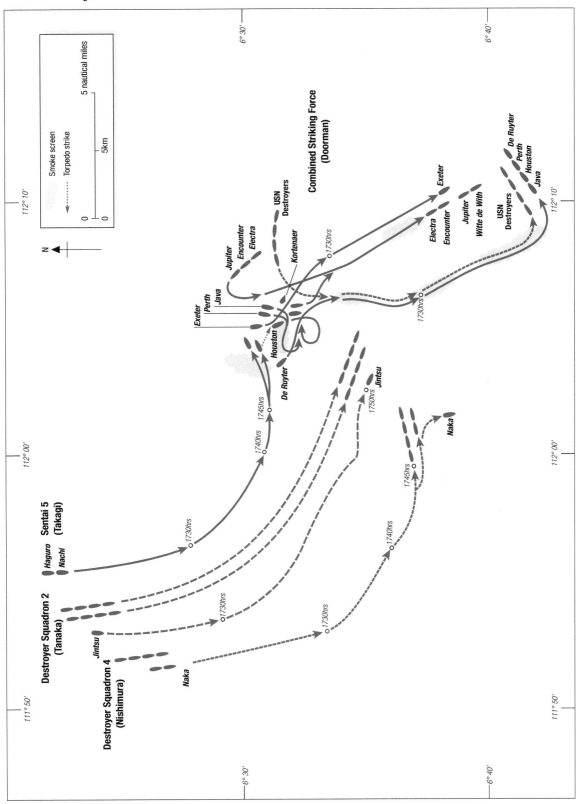

Smoke screen

······▶ Torpedo strike

5 nautical miles

5km

N

112° 10'

6° 30'

6° 40'

Combined Striking Force (Doorman)

USN Destroyers

Jupiter
Encounter
Electra

Kortenaer

Exeter

Electra
Encounter

Jupiter
Witte de With

USN Destroyers

De Ruyter
Perth
Houston
Java

1730hrs

1730hrs

Exeter
Perth
Java

Houston

De Ruyter

1745hrs

1740hrs

Jintsu

1750hrs

Naka

1745hrs

Sentai 5 (Takagi)

Haguro
Nachi

1730hrs

Destroyer Squadron 2 (Tanaka)

1730hrs

1740hrs

1730hrs

Jintsu

Destroyer Squadron 4 (Nishimura)

Naka

111° 50'

112° 00'

111° 50'

112° 00'

112° 10'

6° 30'

6° 40'

flagship with a 4.7in. shell which killed one and wounded four. *Encounter* followed *Electra* out of the smoke, and immediately took *Jintsu* under fire. Nishimura's lead destroyers *Asagumo* and *Minegumo* were the closest to the British ships; *Encounter* and *Minegumo* exchanged fire at short range between 1800 and 1810hrs with the Japanese ship taking minor damage. Meanwhile, *Electra* was busy engaging *Asagumo*. The British ship put a shell into *Asagumo*'s engine room from 5,000 yards, which killed four and wounded 19 and brought the Japanese ship to a temporary halt. *Electra*'s luck did not hold. *Asagumo* hit the British ship first on her bridge, and then in a boiler room which caused a loss of power. *Minegumo* then finished off the powerless *Electra*, which sank at 1816hrs. Only 54 of her crew survived, and these were rescued by an American submarine the following day.

In the opening phases of the battle, Doorman's force had suffered minimal damage from the two Japanese mass torpedo attacks, but Japanese gunfire had crippled *Exeter* and *Electra*. Most importantly, the Allied force had made no progress getting to grips with the invasion convoy. With the Japanese floatplanes providing constant updates to Takagi, it appeared unlikely that Doorman could find an opening to close with the convoy. In spite of his increasingly unfavorable situation, Doorman continued to press his attack. After re-forming his cruiser force with *De Ruyter* leading *Perth*, *Houston*, and *Java*, he headed to the east and placed his force between the Japanese and *Exeter*. Since *Exeter* could not exceed 15 knots, even after the best efforts of her engine room crew to make repairs, Doorman ordered her to return to Soerabaja escorted by *Witte De With*. She arrived there without further incident.

With darkness approaching, Doorman needed to break contact with the Japanese to find a new path to attack the invasion convoy under

This is light cruiser *Perth* in a pre-war photograph. Along with sister ships *Hobart* and *Sydney*, these were well-balanced and modern ships. However, they were outclassed by the IJN's much larger and more powerful heavy cruisers. (Netherlands Institute for Military History)

Battle of the Java Sea: Third Phase, 1750–1820hrs

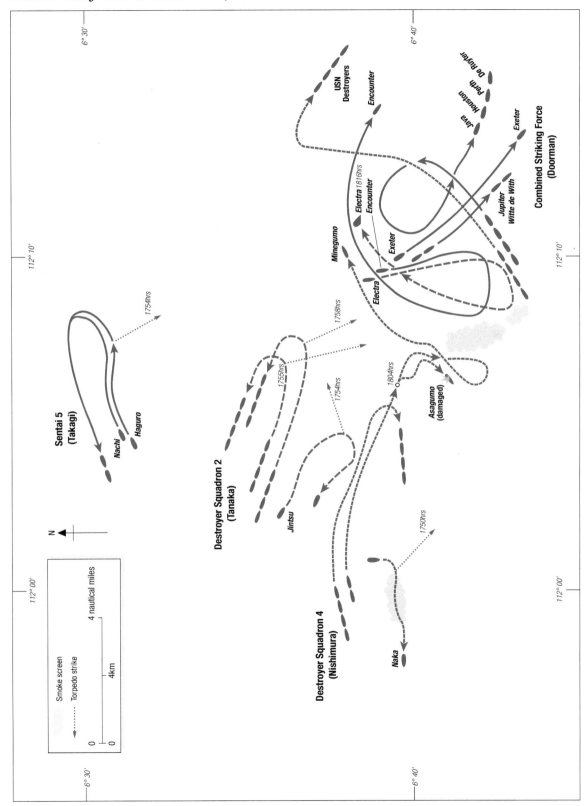

Naka, shown here after being torpedoed on April 1, 1942 by US Navy submarine *Seawolf* off Christmas Island, served as Rear Admiral Nishimura's flagship during the NEI campaign. She missed the battle of Balikpapan because of Nishimura's poor force deployment, but did participate in the battle of the Java Sea. She was sunk later in the war in February 1944, during the US Navy's massive carrier raid on IJN forces at Truk Atoll. (Yamato Museum)

the cloak of darkness. With this in mind, Doorman sent an order to the four American destroyers to attack at 1806hrs. This order was quickly cancelled, but the Americans were subsequently ordered to lay smoke, and finally to cover Doorman's retirement. Thoroughly confused, the officers on the flagship *John D. Edwards* decided to make a torpedo attack. The four four-stackers headed toward the Japanese at 28 knots. Unwilling to get too close to *Nachi* and *Haguro*, the four American destroyers launched 20 torpedoes from their starboard tubes at 1817hrs, and then reversed course and fired 21 port-side torpedoes. The torpedoes were launched at ranges of 10,000–13,000 yards, near maximum range for the Mark 8. Takagi cautiously decided to turn his cruisers to the north; all of the torpedoes missed.

In the remaining daylight, Takagi assessed his next move. Doorman's force was headed to the east, apparently returning to base. The explosions of many torpedoes, which were actually Type 93s exploding prematurely, indicated heavy Allied losses. The Japanese had moved close to the shore of Java, and Takagi wanted to avoid running into a Dutch minefield. The battle appeared over, so Takagi ordered his combatants north to regroup and for the convoy to head south to its landing area.

Doorman had taken losses, but remained determined to get at the invasion convoy. At 1831hrs, he changed course to the northeast. He had no information on the location of the convoy, but presumed it to be somewhere to his north. His force had been whittled down to the four remaining cruisers, the destroyer *Jupiter* and the four American destroyers, none of which had any torpedoes remaining and all of which were running low on fuel.

Battle of the Java Sea: Fourth Phase, 1900–1950hrs

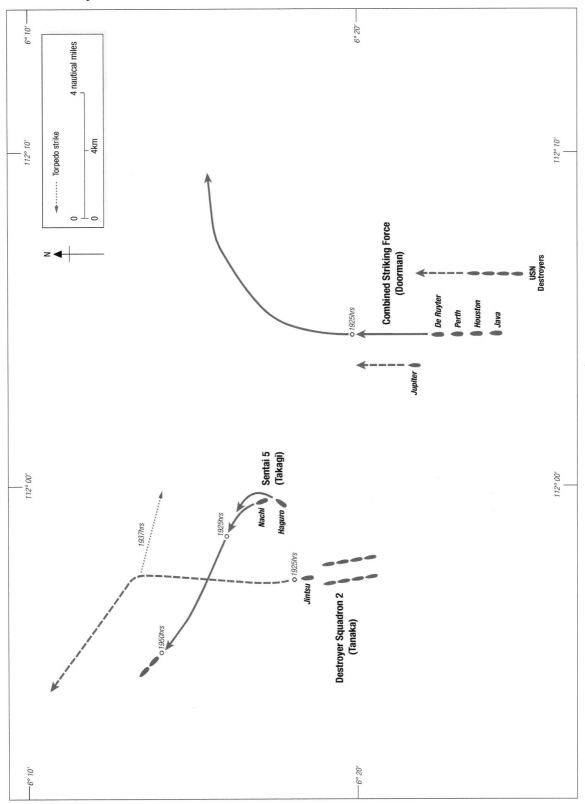

The night phase

The change of course by the Combined Striking Force was reported to Takagi within minutes of it occurring, this time by an aircraft from *Jintsu*. Takagi tried to reassemble his force to meet Doorman's thrust. This took a while since the various destroyer divisions were spread all over in the aftermath of the massed torpedo attack. The last of Tanaka's three divisions were not rounded up until 1907hrs. Two of Nishimura's destroyers, *Asagumo* and *Minegumo*, both of which were damaged, headed off to join the convoy and were out of the fight.

Doorman's move to the north temporarily caught Takagi off guard. At 1904hrs, he ordered the convoy to again move to the north to escape danger. More dangerously, *Nachi* and *Haguro* were in the process of recovering their floatplanes, which meant they had come to a stop and were potentially vulnerable. The Japanese cruisers were not spotted in this condition from 1857 to 1922hrs, and once underway again lookouts aboard the cruisers spotted the Allied formation to the southeast. Tanaka's squadron stumbled briefly into a position between the two cruiser forces and came under fire at 1933hrs from *Houston* and *Perth*. *Jintsu* replied with four torpedoes, which missed.

Still determined to get through to the transports, Doorman changed course to the east with the intent of coming south toward the coast to get around the Japanese. At 2100hrs, he was headed again to the west. At this point, the commander of the four American destroyers, Commander Thomas H. Binford, decided to take his ships and head back to Soerabaja only some 50 miles to the east. His stated reason was that he was out of torpedoes and almost out of fuel. In addition, Binford was wary of following Doorman into an impossible fight. Of all the ships which began under Doorman's command

The most powerful Allied destroyer in the campaign, the British *Jupiter*, was sunk by a drifting Dutch mine. The explosion occurred in one of the ship's engine rooms, which flooded the room and the boilers and caused a loss of power. Slow flooding sank the ship four hours later with the loss of 70 crewmen. (Netherlands Institute for Military History)

Battle of the Java Sea: Fifth Phase, 2300–2400hrs

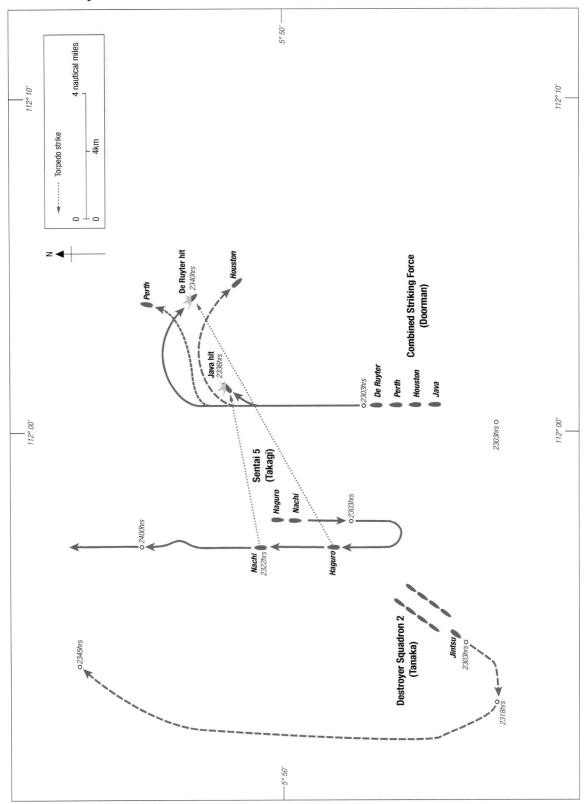

Torpedo strike

4 nautical miles

4km

N

Perth

De Ruyter hit
2340hrs

Houston

Java hit
2336hrs

2303hrs

De Ruyter
Perth
Houston
Java

Combined Striking Force
(Doorman)

Sentai 5
(Takagi)

Haguro
Nachi

2303hrs

2400hrs

Nachi
2322hrs

Haguro

2345hrs

Destroyer Squadron 2
(Tanaka)

Jintsu

2303hrs

2318hrs

112° 10'

112° 00'

112° 10'

112° 00'

5° 50'

5° 50'

The crew of *De Ruyter* pictured on the quay at the Soerabaja naval base. Of her crew of 437, 235 were lost when the ship was hit by a single torpedo. When the crew was ordered to abandon ship, it did so in a chaotic way, and many were lost even though it took the ship two and a half hours to sink after being torpedoed. (Netherlands Institute for Military History)

on the morning of February 27, only Binford's four destroyers were still afloat on the evening of March 2.

The departure of the American destroyers left only five ships under Doorman's command – the four cruisers and *Jupiter*. Destroyer *Encounter* was straggling behind, trying to catch up. A floatplane from *Naka* had relieved *Jintsu*'s aircraft and used flares to mark the progress of the Allied force. More bad luck dogged the Allies. At 2125hrs, just as Doorman was leading his force north in a final attempt to find the transports, *Jupiter* hit a Dutch mine. The ship lost power, and foundered hours later.

The Allied force continued north in its vain search for the invasion convoy. At this point both sides were exhausted and low on ammunition. *Perth* had only 160 6in. rounds remaining, and *Houston* was down to some 300 8in. shells. Doorman refused to consider breaking off the action, but the battle would soon come to an end whether he wanted it to or not. At 2200hrs, Takagi lost radio contact with *Naka*'s floatplane, leaving him blind for the first time in the battle. He nervously steered a course to the south with his two heavy cruisers and ordered his two destroyer squadrons to join him. Not until 2302hrs did a lookout on *Nachi* spot Doorman's column some 16,000 yards to the southeast. The Japanese cruisers turned north to assume a parallel track and prepared to make a torpedo attack. The Allied cruisers spotted Takagi's ships at 2310hrs and opened fire. The Japanese returned a slow fire at 2321hrs. They had only one-third of their 8in. shells remaining, but the Japanese did have enough Type 93 torpedoes for a final salvo. This was launched at 2322hrs with *Nachi* contributing eight torpedoes and *Haguro* four. The range was some 14,000 yards. Doorman made an attempt to maneuver in expectation of a torpedo attack, but it was too late.

Two of the 12 torpedoes hit. At 2336hrs, a Type 93 from *Nachi* hit *Java* aft. The impact of the 1,078-pound warhead caused the aft magazine to explode which blew off some 100 feet of the cruiser's stern. Given the cruiser's inadequate internal compartmentation, this was a fatal blow. The crew was ordered to abandon ship, and within 15 minutes of being hit, *Java* sank with the loss of all but 19 of her crew of 528. Probably thinking that the torpedo threat had passed, *De Ruyter* made a turn to starboard exposing her broadside to the four torpedoes from *Haguro*. One hit aft and created a large fire that engulfed the entire stern portion of the ship. Power was also lost, which made it impossible to put out the fire. *De Ruyter* sank during the night at 0230hrs along with 344 men. Among the casualties was Doorman, who refused to leave the ship.

With these crushing blows, the battle came to an end. *Houston* and *Perth* changed course and headed to the southeast. No attempt was made to rescue the survivors of the Dutch cruisers per Doorman's orders that there should be no attempt made to rescue survivors. The Japanese destroyers attempted to engage the remaining Allied ships, but were unable to do so in the smoke and confusion. The following day at noon, the two surviving ships arrived at Tanjong Priok.

THE ALLIED ROUT IS COMPLETE

As Doorman's Eastern Striking Force was being defeated, what became of the Allied Western Striking Force? The detachment of *Exeter*, *Perth*, and three destroyers left it with only three light cruisers (two obsolete) and three (two obsolete) destroyers. On February 26, an RAF aircraft spotted the Japanese invasion force some 100 miles north of Batavia. Helfrich ordered the Western Striking Force to sortie and engage it. The force departed that evening, under the tactical command of the skipper of *Hobart*, and after a half-hearted effort to intercept the Japanese, headed back to base on February 27 short of fuel. By this point, the fate of Java was clear, and the senior British naval officer on Java, Rear Admiral Arthur Palliser, decided that he did not want to sacrifice his ships in a futile defense. He persuaded Helfrich to agree to a withdrawal of his force if it was unable to find the Japanese. Accordingly, Collins crafted orders for his command to patrol in an area where no Japanese were operating until 0430hrs on February 28, and then to depart for Ceylon by the Sunda Strait. Thankfully for the ships concerned, all but the Dutch destroyers were able to transit the Sunda Strait just before the arrival of the Japanese invasion force.

The survivors of Doorman's Combined Striking Force faced a very uncertain future. The two pincers of the Japanese invasion force were now located on both ends of Java, trapping *Perth*, *Houston*, and the Dutch destroyer *Evertsen* in Tanjong Priok. In Soerabaja, the American destroyer *Pope* had been joined by the other Allied survivors of the battle, including the damaged *Exeter*, Dutch destroyer *Witte de With*, the British *Encounter*, and Commander Binford's four destroyers.

DEATH OF *DE RUYTER* (PP. 76–77)

Approaching midnight, Doorman refused to break off the action. At this point, the Allied force consisted of only four cruisers, led by Doorman's flagship *De Ruyter*. This scene shows *De Ruyter* steaming at high speed **(1)**. The ship's four 5.9in. turrets are trained to port and are elevated for long-range fire **(2)**. The action was finally brought to an end by a salvo of 12 Type 93 torpedoes from *Nachi* and *Haguro*. From a range of 14,000 yards, the Japanese torpedoes headed toward the Allied cruiser column. Doorman was slow to respond to this threat. At 2336hrs, a torpedo from

Nachi hit *Java* which blew off the cruiser's stern and caused her to sink with heavy loss of live some 15 minutes later. At about 2340hrs, a single torpedo from *Haguro* hit *De Ruyter* aft **(3)**. The Type 93 with its powerful warhead hit the starboard aft engine room as shown in this view. The ship lost power and coasted to a stop. Within 30 minutes, the captain ordered the crew to abandon ship. The starboard list increased until the ship sank some two and a half hours later. The torpedo hit on *De Ruyter* brought one of the longest surface battles of the Pacific War to an end.

The perilous Allied situation meant the end to the fragile ABDA command structure. February 25 was ABDA's final official day. Now the Allies began to pursue different objectives. Helfrich retained nominal control over all Allied naval ships in the region, and he clung to the increasingly unrealistic notion that Java could still be defended. He ordered all survivors to Tjilatjap on Java's southern coast to fight on. On March 1, Palliser made clear his intention to order all British ships out of the region before they were destroyed. With no orders to withdraw the US Navy's remaining ships, Glassford indicated to Helfrich that he would keep his ships under Dutch command.

THE BATTLE OF THE SUNDA STRAIT

The first of a series of desperate battles fought by Allied ships seeking to flee the Java Sea was fought on February 28 in the Sunda Strait. *Houston* and *Perth* departed Tanjong Priok at 1900hrs on February 28. *Evertsen*, also present, did not get underway until 2045hrs. The three ships headed west to transit the Sunda Strait. But the Allies were too slow. The large Japanese invasion force had already arrived at Bantam Bay, which was at the northern entrance of the Sunda Strait. Despite their awareness of the presence of Allied warships in Batavia, Rear Admiral Hara, commander of the convoy screen, was not prepared for the two Allied cruisers coming from the east. The Japanese initial deployment placed only *Fubuki* to the east of the landing area. Light cruiser *Natori* with Fubuki-class destroyers *Hatsuyuki* and *Shirayuki* and three older Kamikaze-class destroyers were

This Japanese wartime painting shows *Houston* under attack at the battle of the Sunda Strait. The Japanese destroyer in the foreground is one of the three Kamikaze-class ships present and the crew is servicing the twin torpedo launchers fitted on those ships. The image is fairly accurate in that the battle was a melee fought at close range. (US Naval History and Heritage Command)

Battle of the Sunda Strait, February 28 to March 1

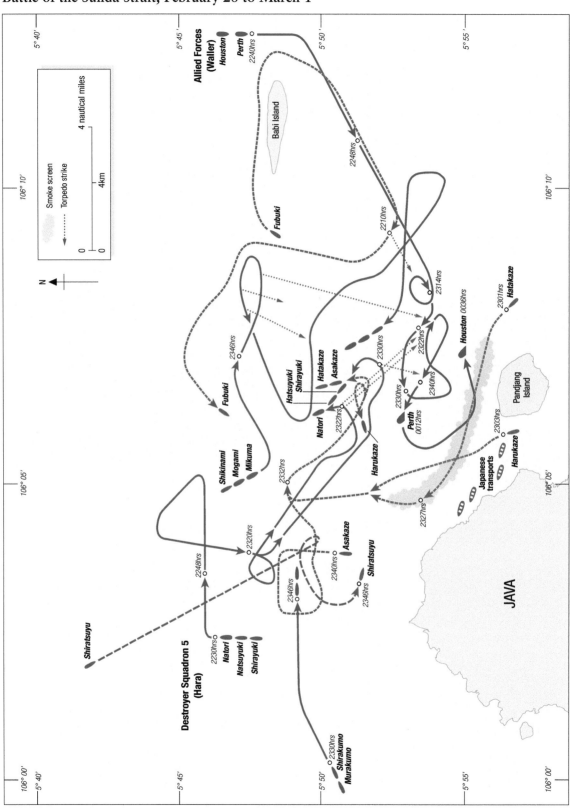

Allied Forces (Waller)
Houston
Perth
2240hrs

Babi Island

2248hrs

Fubuki

2210hrs

2314hrs

Houston 0036hrs

Hatakaze

2346hrs

Fubuki

2330hrs

Hatsuyuki
Shirayuki
Hatakaze
Asakaze

2330hrs

2322hrs

2340hrs

Natori

2321hrs

Perth
0012hrs

Shikinami
Mogami
Mikuma

Pandjang Island

2320hrs

2332hrs

Harukaze

2303hrs

Japanese transports

Harukaze

2327hrs

JAVA

2248hrs

2346hrs

2340hrs

Asakaze

Shiratsuyu

Shiratsuyu

2346hrs

Destroyer Squadron 5 (Hara)

2230hrs
Natori
Natsuyuki
Shirayuki

2330hrs
Shirakumo
Murakumo

N

Smoke screen
Torpedo strike

4 nautical miles

4km

5° 40'
5° 45'
5° 50'
5° 55'

106° 00'
106° 05'
106° 10'

providing close escort. Heavy cruisers *Mikuma* and *Mogami*, and another Fubuki-class destroyer *Shikinami* were located 20 miles north of Bantam Bay. Further north in the Java Sea were heavy cruisers *Kumano* and *Suzuya*, two more Fubuki-class destroyers, and light carrier *Ryujo*. If the Japanese could concentrate their forces, the two Allied cruisers faced impossible odds. Making matters worse was the fact that *Houston* still had only some 300 8in. shells on board, and *Perth* only 160 6in. shells.

The Japanese initial deployment was poor, and suggested they were already taking their enemy too lightly following a string of victories. Only *Fubuki* was deployed to the east, even though the Japanese knew that two cruisers were located in Tandjong Priok earlier in the day. The ships best suited to handle this potential threat, the four heavy cruisers of Kurita's Sentai 7, patrolled north of the landing area. The ironic result was that the two exhausted and low on ammunition Allied cruisers found themselves in an ideal position to attack a major Japanese invasion convoy just as it was in the process of landing its troops. Hara was forced to scramble when first contact was reported on the two cruisers, but had the Allied ships been able to seize the opportunity, the result could have been disastrous for the Japanese. When the Japanese did react to the presence of the two cruisers, they responded in a chaotic way, sinking five of their own ships in the process and taking a considerable amount of time to finally sink the two intruders. On the surface, the result of the battle of the Sunda Strait indicated yet another Japanese victory, but in fact, the IJN's performance was probably its worst of the war to date.

The hopes of the Allied cruiser crews to make an undetected transit of the Sunda Strait were dashed when at 2239hrs *Fubuki* spotted the Allied ships 11,000 yards to the east. Hara reacted with *Natori*, *Hatsuyuki*, and *Shirayuki*. At 2248hrs, *Natori* spotted two ships to the southeast. Hara decided the two ships were cruisers, so he called for additional reinforcements in the form of *Mikuma*, *Mogami*, and destroyers *Harukaze*, *Hatakaze*, and *Asakaze*. Hara further decided he would draw the two enemy cruisers away from the invasion convoy using *Natori* as a target before committing his two heavy cruisers. Meanwhile, *Fubuki* had assumed a trailing position some 3,000 yards behind *Houston*.

As the various groups of Japanese ships converged on the two cruisers, the Allied ships never got an accurate picture of the size of the force they were facing. However, they were aware that the 27-transport Japanese invasion convoy was located to their southwest in Bantam Bay. The ensuing fight was a melee fought at close range and in total confusion for both sides.

The battle opened with *Fubuki* firing a full salvo of nine Type 90 torpedoes (not all Japanese destroyers were carrying the Type 93) at the Allied cruisers at 2314hrs. The target angle was poor, and no hits were scored. The destroyer also fired 16 rounds of 5in. shells, all for no effect. A minute later, *Perth* sighted destroyer *Harukaze* to the southwest and opened fire. As the two cruisers maneuvered, it was apparent that Hara's plan to use *Natori* as bait was not working, so he ordered his destroyers to attack. The first to do so were *Hatsuyuki* and *Shirayuki* at about 2340hrs. *Perth* hit the charging *Shirayuki* on her bridge, but the Japanese destroyers closed to 4,000 yards before each firing nine torpedoes. The old destroyers of Destroyer Division 5 were next. *Harukaze* was hit by several shells and forced out of line. *Asakaze* fired six torpedoes at 2343hrs, but the last destroyer, *Hatakaze*, was unable to find a target. At 2344hrs, *Natori* fired four torpedoes and 29 5.5in. rounds before withdrawing north. Once the Japanese destroyers cleared the area, *Mikuma* and *Mogami* each fired six torpedoes at 2346hrs. At 2352hrs, the two Japanese heavy cruisers turned on their searchlights and began to engage targets with their ten 8in. guns. *Houston* used the searchlights as an aiming point and hit *Mikuma* at 2355hrs. None of this wave of Japanese torpedoes hit their targets, and after the first 45 minutes of an intense firefight, the two Allied cruisers had suffered little damage. However, they were increasingly unable to fire back – *Perth* was reduced to firing practice 6in. shells and *Houston*'s crew was forced to move 260-pound 8in. shells from the aft magazine to the two forward turrets by hand.

As the rate of fire from the two Allied cruisers decreased, the Japanese closed for another torpedo attack. From the east at only 4,200 yards, *Harukaze* fired five and *Hatakaze* six torpedoes at 2356hrs. A minute later, *Mogami* fired six Type 93s from 10,000 yards to the north while opening fire with her 8in. battery. *Shirakumo* and *Murakumo* arrived from the west to each fire nine Type 90 torpedoes from a 5,000 yards range. *Natori* had reloaded her torpedoes and fired at *Houston* at a range of some 9,000 yards. This was a deadly barrage, but not entirely in the way the Japanese intended. *Mogami*'s torpedoes missed their intended targets and headed southwest into Bantam Bay. The results against the anchored invasion convoy were devastating. Four torpedoes hit transports, and all sank (but were eventually raised and returned to service). Aboard transport *Ryujo Maru*, General Imamura Hitoshi, commander of the 16th Army, was dumped into the sea and forced to swim for his life. A fifth torpedo hit 600-ton minesweeper *W2* which broke in two and quickly sank.

Action in the Bali Strait, February 28

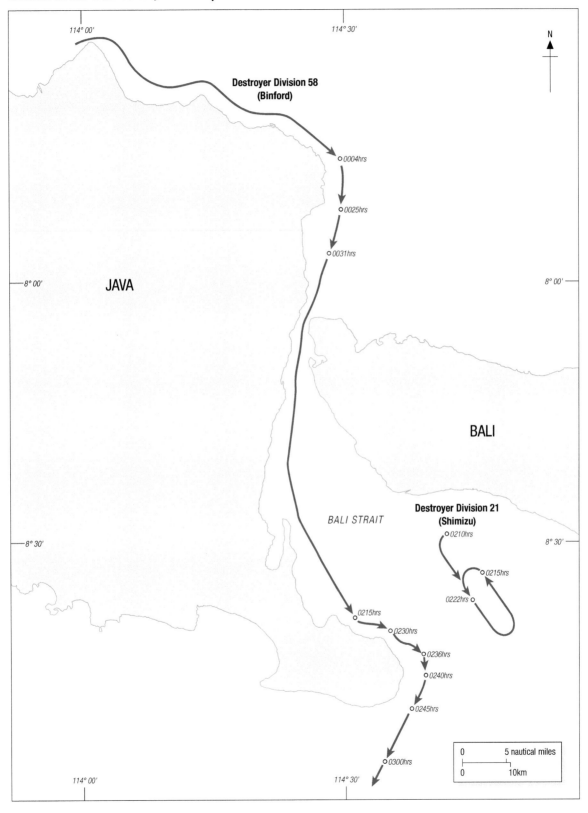

Wakaba was one of six ships in the Hatsuhara class. Four of these were assigned to Destroyer Division 21 and were active in supporting several invasions in the eastern NEI. Their only opportunity to engage Allied ships came on the night of February 28–March 1, when they detected the four ships of the US Navy's Destroyer Division 58 transiting the Bali Strait. Despite having an advantage in speed and firepower, the Japanese ships did not pursue aggressively, and all four American destroyers escaped. (US Naval History and Heritage Command)

More explosions followed, and these were at the expense of the Allies. At about 0005hrs on March 1, a torpedo possibly from *Harukaze* hit *Perth* in her forward engine room. Two minutes later, another hit under the bridge. When the barrage from *Murakumo* and *Shirakumo* arrived, two more hit. Unable to withstand these blows, the cruiser rolled over to port and sank at 0012hrs. Of her crew of 686, 351 went down with the ship, including her commanding officer. Among the survivors, another 106 died in Japanese captivity.

None of the torpedoes hit *Houston*, but she was now alone. Seeing the way to the west blocked, *Houston's* captain steered south. At 0010hrs, her luck finally ran out. Shells from *Mikuma* and *Mogami* began to score, and within minutes the ship was reduced to shambles. The crew recorded three torpedo hits, but the correct number will never be known since in the final chaotic moments it was impossible to distinguish shell from torpedo hits. Her commanding officer ordered abandon ship at 0025hrs, and then was killed by shrapnel. At 0029hrs, *Shikinami* closed to short range for a final torpedo hit, and five minutes later the cruiser disappeared. Of her crew of 1,061, only 368 survived the sinking. Of these, 102 died in Japanese captivity.

A postscript to the destruction of the two Allied cruisers was the fate of *Evertsen*. Seeing the battle in the Sunda Strait from a distance, her commanding officer attempted to head north along the coast of Sumatra. At 0130hrs, the Dutch destroyer was detected by *Murakumo* and *Shirakumo*. In an uneven gun fight, the Japanese destroyers set the Dutch ship afire. Her commanding officer ran the ship aground to save the crew.

Not all was disaster for the Allies. Commander Binford, whose four destroyers were in Soerabaja, was not convinced that the best escape route was through the Sunda Strait. He convinced Glassford to allow him to make a night run through the narrow Bali Strait. Given permission to do so, he departed at 1700hrs on February 28 and entered the Bali Strait at 0200hrs the next morning. Four Hatsuhara-class destroyers were assigned to guard the strait. Hugging the shore along the Java side of the strait, Binford's destroyers were detected and brought under fire from the patrolling Japanese destroyers. On this occasion, the Japanese did not display a killer instinct. The American destroyers replied with their 4in. guns, but neither side hit the other. Binford increased speed to 25 knots, made smoke, and broke out into the Indian Ocean without damage. The next day, no Japanese aircraft appeared, and the four ships arrived in Fremantle on March 4.

Binford's intuition to run the Bali Strait at night had proven correct. After his departure from Soerabaja on the 28th, several Allied ships still remained in port – *Exeter*, *Encounter*, and the American destroyer *Pope*. Palliser did not want to run these through the Bali Strait because of *Exeter*'s draft, and he did not want to use the deep Lombok Strait because an undetected transit seemed unlikely since the Japanese held both sides of the strait, and because the prospects of air attack were great from the airfield on Bali and from Kendari. Incredibly, he ordered the ships to use the Sunda Strait in the hope of catching the Japanese off guard. This order was a death sentence since the prospects of transiting the length of the Java Sea amidst numerous Japanese ships and constant air patrols to even get to the Sunda Strait was remote.

Ikazuchi, a Group III Special Type destroyer, is pictured here underway in Chinese waters about 1938. She was active in the occupation of Ambon, Makassar, and Timor. On March 1, she assisted in the destruction of *Exeter*. (US Naval History and Heritage Command)

THE END OF *EXETER*

Exeter, *Encounter*, and *Pope* departed two hours after Binford and initially headed north before turning to the west. Gaining surprise was

Akebono, a Group II Special Type destroyer shown here in Chinese waters before the war, was active in both the Philippines and Malaya Units during the NEI campaign. She was involved in the final torpedo attacks on *Exeter* on March 1. (US Naval History and Heritage Command)

essential, since *Exeter* had only 20 per cent of her 8in. shells remaining and *Encounter* was without torpedoes. Any hope of gaining surprise was quickly dashed when a Japanese aircraft reported their departure. By 2300hrs, the commanding officer of *Exeter* had learned of the battle in progress in the Sunda Strait. This should have been a red flag, prompting him to ignore his orders and try a new route, but it did not. By morning, the small force was proceeding west in an empty sea and was hopeful of making their escape. Any cause for optimism was smashed when at 0750hrs the British sighted *Nachi* and *Haguro* to the southwest. *Exeter* turned back to the east hoping she had not been seen, but the Japanese were already bringing up additional forces to close the trap. This was Vice Admiral's Takahashi's Support Force with heavy cruisers *Ashigara* and *Myoko*, escorted by destroyers *Akebono* and *Ikazuchi*, which had been held south of Borneo. Now they were given a chance to engage the enemy. At about 0935hrs, they made contact with *Exeter*.

The appearance of four IJN heavy cruisers presented *Exeter*'s skipper with few options. He ordered his small force to steer to the east to escape. The efforts of *Exeter*'s engine room crew had raised her speed to 23 knots, but since this was 10 knots slower than the pursuing Japanese, there was no hope of escape. The action began at 1010hrs with the Allied destroyers exchanging gunfire with *Akebono* and *Ikazuchi*. At 1020hrs, *Ashigara* and *Myoko* joined the fray, targeting *Exeter* from 25,000 yards with the help of a floatplane to correct fire. *Encounter* and *Pope* made smoke to protect *Exeter*, and for the first hour of the action, the Japanese failed to score a hit. However, the Japanese continued to close in, with *Ashigara* and *Myoko* off *Exeter*'s port quarter, and *Nachi* and *Haguro* steaming off her

starboard beam conserving ammunition. Two more destroyers, *Kawakaze* and *Yamakaze*, joined the hunt.

The Allied ships put up a brave fight. *Exeter* and *Pope* fired torpedoes at *Ashigara*, but missed. *Pope* made another torpedo attack, firing four more at *Ashigara*, and five at *Nachi*, but these also missed. By 1115hrs, *Nachi* and

In the photograph taken by a Japanese floatplane, *Exeter* is shown rolling over to starboard and capsizing. Her captain had given the order to scuttle the ship after she had lost power and was no longer able to fight back. (US Naval History and Heritage Command)

The veteran Dutch destroyer *Witte de With* was lost on March 1 when she was scuttled in Soerabaja. She was unable to leave with the *Exeter* group the previous day because she could not get her orders confirmed in time, another example of the weak RNN command and control throughout the campaign. (Netherlands Institute for Military History)

Another disaster to befall the US Navy late in the NEI campaign was the loss of *Langley* on February 27. *Langley* was the US Navy's first aircraft carrier, being commissioned in 1922 and later converted to a seaplane tender in 1936. Though only able to make 13 knots and despite being totally unprotected, she was pressed into service as an aircraft ferry to carry fighter planes to the NEI. Attacked by long-range bombers south of Tjilatjap, she suffered five hits and three near misses in an attack by nine IJN bombers. She was abandoned, and was later torpedoed by destroyer *Whipple*, as shown here. (US Naval History and Heritage Command)

Haguro had closed to 17,000 yards and opened fire with their main battery. Beginning at 1119hrs, *Nachi*, *Haguro*, *Kawakaze*, and *Yamakaze* all fired four torpedoes, but all missed. Then the crippling blow came at 1120hrs in the form of an 8in. shell which hit *Exeter* in one of her boiler rooms. This hit was even worse than that suffered at Java Sea; the cruiser lost power which meant she could neither fight nor flee. The four Japanese cruisers continued to fire 8in. shells at the helpless *Exeter* and fired additional torpedoes. The only Japanese torpedoes to hit came from *Ikazuchi*, and these only as the British were abandoning ship. The cruiser sank at 1200hrs. On this occasion, the IJN was merciful and picked up 651 of the crew.

The two Allied destroyers did not survive. *Encounter* suffered an unfortunate near miss by an 8in. shell at 1135hrs which led to the evacuation

This Japanese photo shows heavy shells bursting around destroyer *Edsall* on March 1. Under its skipper Lt. Joshua Nix, the well-handled ship evaded the gunfire of heavy cruisers *Tone* and *Chikuma* (firing 844 8in. and 62 5in. rounds) and battleships *Hiei* and *Kirishima* (firing 297 14in. and 132 6in. rounds) for over an hour until the intervention of dive-bombers from the Kido Butai sealed the destroyer's fate. (US Naval History and Heritage Command)

of the engine room and the ship going dead in the water. The destroyer's skipper ordered his crew to abandon ship and the ship scuttled. Again, the Japanese were merciful and 149 were rescued. *Pope* survived another few hours by heading into a rain squall. This succeeded in losing the Japanese surface ships, but at 1300hrs Japanese aircraft located the destroyer heading north to Borneo. Ten F1M "Pete" floatplanes dropped 132-pound bombs, followed by six B5N1s from *Ryujo* with 550-pound bombs. *Pope* avoided every bomb, but a near miss put one of the propeller shafts out of commission and caused progressive flooding. The skipper ordered the ship scuttled, which was well under way by the time *Myoko* and *Ashigara* showed up. The destroyer sank at 1420hrs. Two days later, 150 men of her crew were picked up by a Japanese destroyer.

There were other Allied ships trying to flee from Java. One was destroyer *Edsall*, which had the misfortune of being sighted by the Kido Butai on March 1. It took two battleships and two heavy cruisers, assisted by 17 dive-bombers, 84 minutes to sink the well-handled destroyer. Eight survivors were rescued, but all were beheaded at Kendari after being sent ashore. The following day, heavy cruiser *Maya* and two destroyers sank the British destroyer *Stronghold* and that evening, heavy cruisers *Atago* and *Takao* sank American destroyer *Pillsbury* southeast of Tjilatjap. In all, the Japanese sank or captured 20 Allied naval and merchant ships fleeing from Java Destroyers *Whipple* and *Parrott*, and lesser ships of the Asiatic Fleet successfully reached Australia. The naval campaign for the NEI was over.

This shot from about 1930 shows *Pillsbury* steaming at high speed. The Asiatic Fleet's flush-deck destroyers were unmodified from their original configuration with a principal armament of four single 4in. mounts and four triple torpedo mounts. (US Naval History and Heritage Command)

ANALYSIS

At the start of the campaign, the RNN had 12 operational subs in the NEI and three more in overhaul or reserve. This is *K-XIII* photographed in 1924, which dated from the 1918 Naval Program and only carried six torpedoes. Like the more numerous US Navy submarines, Dutch subs were also ineffective attacking Japanese amphibious forces in the NEI. Four Dutch subs were lost during the campaign. In the final days of the campaign *K-X*, *K-XIII*, and *K-XVIII* were trapped in Soerabaja and scuttled. (US Naval History and Heritage Command)

The battle of the Java Sea was one of the largest surface battles of the Pacific War. A total of 32 ships took part, and of these five were sunk, all Allied, and another eight damaged (two Allied and six Japanese). In addition to Java Sea, there were four other major surface actions fought during the campaign. In only one of these, Balikpapan, could the Allies be considered victorious. The overall losses for each side tell the story. Of the Dutch Navy's three cruisers and seven destroyers available at the start of the campaign, only light cruiser *Tromp* remained afloat. The Asiatic Fleet's losses were considerable, but not as drastic. Three cruisers began the war, and two (*Boise* and *Marblehead*) survived, though both were damaged. Seven of the fleet's 13 destroyers also survived. Both navies had fought with determination, but for little effect. Though the Royal Navy never supported the defense of the NEI with the same dedication as the Dutch and Americans, it also suffered heavily. British losses totaled one heavy cruiser and four destroyers. The Australians lost a light cruiser.

The IJN had accomplished the utterly essential mission of seizing the NEI and its critical resource facilities quickly. In so doing, no Japanese landing was halted or even delayed. There were occasions when sloppy tactical dispositions provided the Allies with the chance of inflicting local reverses, but the Allies were too unlucky or weak to take advantage of them. Japanese naval losses were light during the campaign. Allied surface naval units did

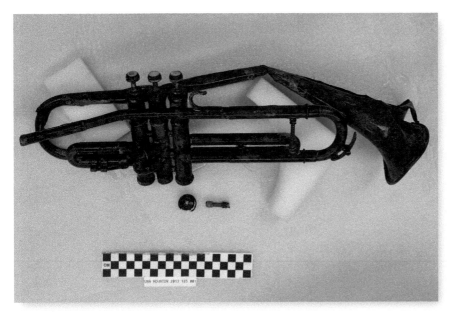

This trumpet was recovered from the USS *Houston*. The ship is a war grave, but in recent years there has been a very disturbing trend of Indonesian scrappers salvaging war wrecks in the former NEI. While *Houston* remains apparently in good shape, some of the other ships like *Perth* and the American and British destroyers are almost entirely gone. (US Naval History and Heritage Command)

not sink a single large IJN combatant during the campaign, and only at Balikpapan did Allied surface ships sink anything. The Dutch accounted for the majority of the Japanese transports and combatants lost during the campaign, but these losses were far below what the Japanese planned for. The largest combatant lost by the Japanese in the NEI was a destroyer. Three were lost – one to an American submarine, one to a Dutch submarine, and the third to Dutch aircraft. Other losses included one submarine, four minesweepers, and a patrol boat. In addition, at least 14 transports were sunk.

At the operational level, both sides made serious errors. At the Badoeng Strait, Helfrich was caught off guard and his plan was too complicated. In the run-up to the Japanese invasion of Java, Helfrich was foolish to think that he could repel both the eastern and western Japanese thrusts against Java, and his creation of two striking forces further dissipated his already inadequate assets. His only hope for success was to create a single powerful striking force and make all efforts to provide it with adequate air reconnaissance and air cover. He failed to ensure that the remaining Allied air assets on Java were focused on support of the Combined Striking Force. Had adequate aerial reconnaissance supported a strengthened striking force, it might have been possible to deliver the Japanese a serious blow, maybe even strong enough to delay or defeat one of the landing forces. None of this is to say that the Allies ever had a real chance to defend Java from seaborne invasion. The balance of forces, both quantitatively and qualitatively, was too uneven. In the final analysis, the record of Allied naval forces in the campaign, culminating in the battle of the Java Sea, was a parade of defeats. The only exception was at the opening battle at Balikpapan, when bold action created surprise and delivered the Allies a local success. Even so, it should be pointed out that even this success resulted in no delay in the Japanese timetable for conquering the NEI.

The Japanese deployed their naval forces poorly during the campaign, thus creating possible openings for the Allies. In spite of the fact that the Eastern Force was operating nearest to the principal Allied naval base at

Soerabaja, it was significantly weaker than the Western Force. The Japanese compounded this error in the later stages of the campaign by dissipating their overwhelming resources. Yamamoto took reports from the battle of the Badoeng Strait literally and assumed that ABDA no longer possessed a viable striking force. Accordingly, instead of supporting the final invasion of Java with the overwhelming force of the Kido Butai and the battleships and heavy cruisers of Kondo's support force to deal with any potential Allied naval intervention, he deployed these forces into the Indian Ocean to pick off ships fleeing Java. This left the weakest of the four main Japanese forces in the region to contend with the main Allied naval force, Doorman's Combined Striking Force. This propensity of Yamamoto's to disperse his forces was of no major significance when the odds were so heavily stacked in the IJN's favor, but they would become a major factor in major defeats only months later.

Throughout the campaign, Allied tactical performance was weak in all areas. They were never able to address the difficulties of maneuvering a multi-national force and communications remained a critical weakness. Not a single major Japanese naval unit was sunk in surface combat during the campaign. Allied gunnery was atrocious, resulting in few hits. Torpedo reliability and performance was a crippling disadvantage, and this was to continue throughout 1942.

Tactically, the naval battles for the NEI demonstrated the prowess of the Japanese. The Japanese ships were superior on a unit basis, and this proved critical on several occasions. The actions of only two Japanese destroyers provided a tactical victory against a much larger Allied force at the Badoeng Strait. At Java Sea, the two sides were at approximate parity, but the two Japanese heavy cruisers engaged provided enough backbone to defeat one of the largest Allied forces assembled during the campaign. Though the Japanese emerged victorious at Java Sea, there were some causes for concern. Foremost of these was the performance of the IJN's supposed war-winning secret weapon, the Type 93 torpedo. Of the 153 torpedoes fired, only three hit with dozens detonating prematurely. This was a rough start for the Type 93, but the foundation of a long-range torpedo operated by well-drilled crews paid rich dividends later in the war. Even so, the three weapons that hit did account for three Allied ships, including two cruisers, and were responsible for bringing the battle to an end.

Japanese gunnery was also disappointing. Pre-war doctrine called for long-range fire, since the Japanese believed they could deliver punishing blows beyond the reach of their enemies. In pre-war exercises, they assessed that 6 percent of

This is another view of the demise of *Exeter*. Destroyer *Inazuma* picked up most of the survivors, which included 44 officers and 607 men. (US Naval History and Heritage Command)

8in. shells would hit at long range. This proved wildly optimistic, since at Java Sea only five of the 1,619 8in. shells fired hit their target. As was the case with the Type 93, the low accuracy rate was mitigated by the fact that one of the shells that hit played a major role in determining the battle's result. Light cruiser gunnery by *Naka* and *Jintsu* was also poor with only a single round of the 221 5.5in. rounds hitting. Destroyer gunnery was better since it was conducted at shorter range. Of the 515 5in. rounds expended, several hit *Electra* and led to her loss. Similar results were in evidence in the action against *Exeter*. Of 1,171 8in. rounds fired, two hit. Of 35 torpedoes fired, only one hit.

The failure of the Combined Striking Force to stop the Japanese invasion forces meant the Japanese were able to land at three places on Java on February 28 and March 1. Dutch attempts to contain the landings were futile. By March 8, Soerabaja was captured, and the following day Dutch forces on Java surrendered. With the surrender of Dutch troops on Sumatra on March 28, the entire NEI passed to Japanese control. The Japanese had succeeded in accomplishing their most important early-war objective. The oilfields on Java and Sumatra were quickly brought back on line. They were sufficient for Japan's wartime needs, but as the war dragged on the Japanese were increasingly unable to move the oil or refined products to the Home Islands. Java and the great majority of the NEI remained in Japanese hands throughout the war.

BIBLIOGRAPHY AND FURTHER READING

The NEI campaign used to be forgotten when it came to accounts published in English. However, in recent years, many new titles have been issued which have gone a long way to redress this shortcoming. Among these are several featuring extensive use of Dutch sources. Most importantly, the two volumes of the 102-volume *Senshi Sosho* (War History Series – the "official" Japanese history of the war) which deal with the invasion of the NEI have been translated into English. This is the first time any volume of this series has been translated into English in its entirety.

Alford, Lodwick H., *Playing for Time*, Merriam Press, Bennington, Vermont (2012)

Boer, P. C., *The Loss of Java*, NUS Press, Singapore (2011)

Campbell, John, *Naval Weapons of World War Two*, Naval Institute Press, Annapolis, Maryland (1985)

Cox, Jeffrey R., *Rising Sun, Falling Skies*, Osprey Publishing, Oxford (2014)

Dull, Paul S., *A Battle History of the Imperial Japanese Navy (1941–1945)* Naval Institute Press, Annapolis, Maryland (1978)

Foreign Histories Division, General Headquarters Far East Command, *Japanese Monograph No. 101, Naval Operations in the Invasion of Netherlands East Indies December 1941–March 1942*, Tokyo (1950)

Kehn, Donald M., *In the Highest Degree Tragic*, Potomac Books (2017)

Lenton, H. T., *Royal Netherlands Navy*, MacDonald, London (1968)

Leutze, James, *A Different Kind of Victory*, Naval Institute Press, Annapolis, Maryland (1981)

Lohnstein, Marc, *Royal Netherlands East Indies Army 1936–42*, Osprey Publishing, Oxford (2018)

Morison, Samuel E., *The Rising Sun in the Pacific, Volume Three, History of United States Naval Operations in World War II*, Little, Brown and Company, Boston (1975)

O'Hara, Vincent P., *The U.S. Navy Against the Axis*, Naval Institute Press, Annapolis, Maryland (2007)

Rohwer, Jurgen, *Chronology of the War at Sea 1939–1945* (Third Edition), Naval Institute Press, Annapolis, Maryland (2005)

Stille, Mark, *Imperial Japanese Navy Destroyers 1919–45 (1)*, Osprey Publishing, Oxford (2013)

Stille, Mark, *Imperial Japanese Navy Destroyers 1919–45 (2)*, Osprey Publishing, Oxford (2013)

Stille, Mark, *Imperial Japanese Navy Light Cruisers 1941–45*, Osprey Publishing, Oxford (2011)

Stille, Mark, *Imperial Japanese Navy Heavy Cruisers 1941–45*, Osprey Publishing, Oxford (2011)

Thomas, David, *The Battle of the Java Sea*, Stein and Day, New York (1969)

Van Oosten F. C., *The Battle of the Java Sea*, Naval Institute Press, Annapolis, Maryland (1976)

War History Office of the National Defense College of Japan, *The Operations of the Navy in the Dutch East Indies and the Bay of Bengal*, Corts Foundation/Leiden University Press, Netherlands (2018)

War History Office of the National Defense College of Japan, *The Invasion of the Dutch East Indies*, Corts Foundation/Leiden University Press, Netherlands (2015)

Williams, Greg H., *The Last Days of the United States Asiatic Fleet*, McFarland and Company, Jefferson, North Carolina (2018)

Willmott, H. P., *Empires in the Balance*, Naval Institute Press, Annapolis, Maryland (1982)

Winslow, W. G., *The Fleet the Gods Forgot*, Naval Institute Press, Annapolis, Maryland (1982)

Womack, Tom, *The Allied Defense of the Malay Barrier 1941–1942*, McFarland and Company, Jefferson, North Carolina (2016)

Womack, Tom, *The Dutch Naval Air Force Against Japan*, McFarland and Company, Jefferson, North Carolina (2006)

INDEX

Page numbers in **bold** refer to illustrations and their captions.

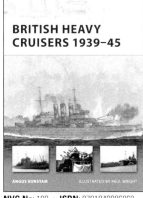

Accounts of history's greatest conflicts, detailing the comma
strategies, tactics and battle experiences of the opposing
forces throughout the crucial stages of each campaign

JAVA SEA 1942

Japan's conquest of the Netherlands East Indies

The battle of the Java Sea, fought in February 1942, was the first major
surface engagement of the Pacific War and one of the few naval battle
of the entire war fought to a decisive victory. It was the culminating
point of the Japanese drive to occupy the Netherlands East Indies (NEI
To defend the NEI, the Allies assembled a striking force comprised of
Dutch, American, British, and even an Australian ship, all under the
command of a resolute Dutch admiral.

On February 27, 1942, the Allied striking force set course to intercept t
Japanese invasion force in the Java Sea. For over seven hours, the Allie
force attempted to attack the Japanese invasion force. In the first phas
both sides engaged in a long-range gunnery duel. After a prolonged lu
the Allied force, now reduced to just four cruisers, attempted another
attack on the invasion convoy during which Japanese torpedoes
scored heavily, sinking two Dutch cruisers and bringing the battle to
a conclusion. Over the next two days, as the Allies attempted to flee,
five more ships were sunk. From that point on, Allied naval power was
eliminated from Southeast Asia and the vast natural resources of the
Netherlands East Indies lay open to the Japanese.

Full color battlescenes ▪ Illustrations ▪ 3-dimensional 'bird's-eye-views' ▪ Maps

UK £16.99   US $25.00   CAN $33.00

ISBN 978-1-4728-3161-3

90300

OSPREY
PUBLISHING

9 781472 831613

THE M4 CARBINE

CHRIS McNAB

Author

Chris McNab is an author and editor specializing in military history and military technology. He has published more than 100 books, including many for Osprey. Chris has also written extensively for major encyclopedia series, magazines, and newspapers.

Illustrators

Johnny Shumate began his career in 1987 after graduating from Austin Peay State University, and now works as a freelance illustrator. Most of his work is rendered in Adobe Photoshop using a Cintiq monitor. His greatest influences are Angus McBride, Don Troiani, and Édouard Detaille. Johnny completed the battlescenes for this book.

Born in Malaya in 1949, Alan Gilliland spent 18 years as the graphics editor of *The Daily Telegraph*, winning 19 awards in that time. He now writes, illustrates, and publishes fiction (www.ravensquill.com), as well as illustrating for a variety of publishers (alangillilandillustration.blogspot.com). Alan completed the cutaway and reticle illustrations for this book.

Other titles in the series

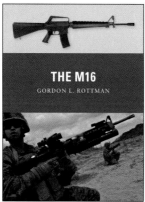

WPN No: 14 • **ISBN:** 9781849086905

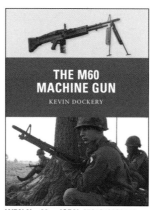

WPN No: 20 • **ISBN:** 9781849088442

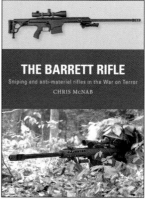

WPN No: 45 • **ISBN:** 9781472811011

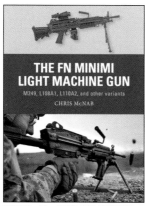

WPN No: 53 • **ISBN:** 9781472816214

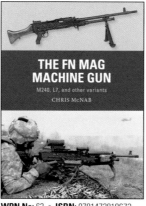

WPN No: 63 • **ISBN:** 9781472819673

WPN No: 69 • **ISBN:** 9781472833099